Detox

Rosalyn Patrick

D0943119

STRATHEARN

This edition published 2003 by
STRATHEARN BOOKS LIMITED
Toronto, Canada

© 2002 Geddes & Grosset, David Dale House,
New Lanark, ML11 9DJ, Scotland

Text by Rosalyn Patrick

This edition first published 2003.

ISBN 1 84205 380 9

Printed and bound in the UK

Contents

Introduction

HOW are you? Before you say 'Fine thanks', think for a moment. How are you really? When you wake up in the mornings, do you long to roll over and grab another three hours' sleep? Do you look in the mirror and wonder where that fresh, taut-skinned youth has gone? Do you suck on coffee after coffee all day long yet still feel irritable and exhausted?

Are you, in short, sick and fed-up of feeling sick and fed-up?

If this is you, you are not alone. A large proportion of us feel this way: prey to minor niggling health problems – from bad hair to bloating to biting people's heads off because they're standing between us and the fizzy drinks machine – yet not suffering from a serious medical complaint. Scratch the surface and most of us feel permanently slightly off-colour but not quite sure where we're going wrong.

Is it the stress at work? The car fumes in the atmosphere? The preservatives in our food?

Well yes, it's all of those things. Add in too many cups of coffee, a few sessions in a smoky pub, too many late nights and little or no aerobic exercise and you have a foolproof recipe for continued under-performance in the health department.

So what to do, bar booking yourself into a health spa for the next five years?

Dare you consider a detox?

Before you slam the book shut at the very mention of the d-word, be assured that it needn't involve an ill-advised three-day crash diet featuring colonic irrigation or a celebrity-endorsed herbal drink that smells like compost and costs half a month's wages for a two-week supply. Your doctor would be appalled – and so would your body.

A proper detox is no more and no less than a healthy, natural diet designed to enhance your body's healthy, natural functions. It means saying goodbye to the toxic substances we think help us get through the day, the caffeine, nicotine and sugar, which actually make us feel worse in the long run; and a big hello to fresh fruit and vegetables, lots of water, whole and organic foods, all topped up with a bit of exercise and a regulated sleep pattern.

Easy! And the results speak for themselves. Within days you'll feel refreshed, your energy levels will have increased, your skin will become clearer, your hair glossier and stronger, and your moods highly improved.

And you won't be hungry or forced to drink twig tea once.

Think about it. If your car was rattling to bits and refusing to start in the mornings, you'd take it straight in for a service.

Perhaps it's time to do the same thing for yourself.

On Your Marks ...

WHAT is a detox? Think of a detox as a spring clean of your body: a serious clear-out of all the junk and toxins you've accumulated over the last few months, or even years.

Follow even a short-term detox plan, the Weekend Refresher for instance, and you will feel instantly lighter, have more energy and look better, just as your house does when you finally get around to hauling your old books down to the charity shop, streamlining your wardrobe and giving every corner a serious dusting down.

What you find when you organize your home is

that you want to keep it that way. You find yourself adopting tidier habits and developing a newfound desire to keep everything in order.

The same thing will happen with the detox diet.

Once you start to feel the benefits of weaning yourself from caffeine and junk food, and start to enjoy whole natural foods and moderate regular exercise, not to mention the beautifying effects, you will want to keep things this way.

A detox will improve your well-being in the short term but, if you adopt its lessons of clean living, it could do wonders for your long-term health and fitness too.

How does it work?

If you put the right fuel in your car, it works perfectly. If you put in diesel by mistake, it stops. The same goes for your body. Feed it exactly what it needs and it will do its absolute best by you. Feed it rubbish and it will be too preoccupied trying to digest the latest delivery of refined carbohydrates and sugars to put in any repair and maintenance work.

A proper detox diet doesn't just help the body speed up its waste disposal capabilities, it also provides all the vitamins and nutrients the body needs to repair and strengthen itself.

The liver is of particular importance, being the organ that extracts toxins such as chemical additives, drugs and alcohol from our food and drink and either breaks them down into less harmful substances, stores them or eliminates them.

If it is too busy processing toxic waste, it cannot attend to one of its other main functions – releasing energy. Which is why, when you're suffering from a hangover, you feel extremely lethargic, and why a heavy meal leaves you listless.

If the liver ends up having to store too many unusable toxins over too long a period of time, then you risk liver damage – a medical condition that will affect your whole bodily system, given how central to your health this major organ is.

So take good care of it. The liver is refreshed by fruit and vegetables, worn out by red wine and slabs of fatty beef. A more detailed account of the liver and its functions can be found later in the book.

The kidneys are also crucial in that they process fluids and flush out toxins. You need to drink at least two litres of water a day, three if you work in an office with air conditioning, have central heating at home or do regular exercise which makes you sweat. The athlete Liz McColgan carries a bottle of water with her all the time, sipping at it every time she remembers. Try to get into the habit of doing this too. If you find water too boring, add a dash of lemon juice or some sugar-free cordial but plain old tap water is best.

Drinking plenty of water can also help to prevent

kidney stones, one of the most common renal problems in the UK, affecting more than 40,000 people a year.

What will it do for me?

Initially, you may find that a detox diet makes you feel even worse!

Those who drink a lot of tea and coffee may experience mild headaches over the first day or two without it. You may also feel quite tired as your body has become so dependent on artificial stimulants, but this will pass quickly too, leaving you with more energy than you had before. Other early symptoms include a coated tongue and bad breath; these are simply manifestations of your body's cleansing process and are short-lived. You may also feel slightly irritable to begin with, which is why it is always best to begin your detox over a weekend or holiday.

Soon you will begin to feel more energized, less prone to mood swings, and find it easier both to drop off to sleep at night and get up in the morning.

Your bowel movements will also become more regular, thanks to a sufficient intake of fibre and fluid (constipation is often caused by mild dehydration).

Longer term effects include a clearer complexion.

If you are prone to 'congestion' around the nostrils, caused by blocked pores, you may well find that this clears up. Your skin will feel smoother and less dry as your circulation improves, which will also make your hair and nails stronger and healthier.

Detoxing may also help you if you are trying to conceive, as it will get your body into the best possible working order. Smoking and drinking and eating junk food is off limits when you are pregnant and the same applies at the pre-pregnancy stage.

In the even longer term you may lose weight. Not in the boom and bust way of crash dieting but as part of the gradual process of your body finding its ideal weight – called the 'set point' by dieticians. Though it takes a while, the good news is that weight lost gradually is more likely to stay off – most sudden weight losses are simply caused by a lack of water and weight is quickly regained. Weight lost slowly is much more likely to be a loss of actual fat.

You may even be able to say goodbye to cellulite, that much maligned 'orange peel' skin to which women in particular, even slim, fit women, are almost universally prey to. When your body is working at maximum efficiency, it takes care of everything, even those little fat pockets tucked in beside your hips.

Get Set ...

Changing your diet takes a bit of forethought, which is about more than putting different things in your trolley the next time you're in the supermarket.

Firstly, you have to be motivated. Forcing yourself to

crunch down on greens without any real notion of what you hope to achieve is a recipe for disaster – you'll be back on the Big Macs before you can say knife.

Secondly, you want to know what you're doing and why. Take time to plan what you will be eating in the next week. Think about why you are doing this and what you hope to achieve. Make your goals positive: the reason 'so that I stop feeling so awful' is hardly going motivate you on a wet Wednesday afternoon in November.

Consider what you'll achieve with all this newfound energy – maybe you can improve your performance at work and get a promotion. If you're stuck in a rut and want to break the deadlock, attending to your physical health is one of the best ways to get kick the process into gear. It's amazing what the head can achieve if the body is in good mettle.

Or maybe you want to be more toned and glowing, to recapture some of that long lost pzazz. Maybe you've got a major holiday coming up, a significant anniversary, or you just want to find out what you're like when you're being all you can be.

It's exciting, it's a journey. So make plans.

1 Planning

Have you ever noticed how wonderful newspapers and magazines manage to make diets look? A mouth-watering illustration of beautifully blanched prawns nestling on a bed of lettuce hearts and ripe watermelon served with a dressing of organic bio-yoghurt is enough to make anyone *want* to count calories.

But if you've actually tried one of these diets you will know how complicated and expensive they can be. Eating poached wild salmon for breakfast and fresh fruit salad for lunch *would* make dieting almost a pleasure but who can afford, both in terms of time and money, such extravagance?

The fact is that most of us are overweight because we choose food according to price and the time it takes to prepare. But with a bit of planning, we can change all this. Our mothers and grandmothers, born in an age prior to the mass-marketing of cheap food when frozen pizza and oven chips weren't an option, had to plan how to make the weekly provisions stretch round the table. And so can we.

For instance, if you're going to make salad one lunchtime, plan to have salad again with your evening meal and use the remaining lettuce and tomatoes to spruce up a sandwich for lunch the next day. If you are making crudités, use up the remaining celery and carrot in a soup, or buy a juicer and have the rest at breakfast.

Resist the temptation to buy several bags of apples and oranges in one go, and get into the habit of buying smaller amounts more regularly instead. That way, you always have fresh produce and avoid rotting fruit bowl syndrome. If it looks like you've bought too much, mix up a fruit salad or stew the apples and pears and eat them with breakfast cereal.

The best way to plan is to sit down with a pen and paper before you do your shopping and not just construct a list, but also outline exactly what meals you are going to make, and on what days you are going to make them. This might kill mealtime spontaneity but it also cuts out that oh-my-god-what's-for-dinner-type stress.

Choose easy meals for late nights and more complicated ones for when you have time to spare. Cook in advance and store meal-sized portions in the freezer. Try to avoid slipping ready-meals into your supermarket trolley 'just in case'. If you've got time to wrench a frozen lasagne from its packaging and put it in the microwave, you've probably got time to boil up a little wholewheat pasta while you chop up and sauté an onion, add in some tomatoes, pesto and chopped pepper and season to taste.

Not only is it more satisfying to eat something you have cooked with your own fair hand, it is also much better for you. Even supposedly healthy option pre-cooked foods are packed with salt and sugar and preservatives to make them last and to improve the taste. It may look like a genuine Margarita pizza but be assured, if it comes with its own pre-sealed, microwave-friendly container, it is a feat of chemical engineering rather than culinary art.

Finally, don't forget about herbs and spices, which are a much healthier way of adding taste to a dish than salt. Fresh is by far the best so, if you have a windowsill to spare, why not buy a selection of herb plants so that you always have what you need to hand? Chives, coriander, basil and parsley will cover most eventualities. When using fresh, you need – as a general rule of thumb – about twice the amount you need of dried, which is always more concentrated. When compiling a stock cupboard, buy seasonings as required rather than investing in a whole range, many of which you may never use.

2 Going seasonal ... and organic

Thanks to a huge improvement in transport and refrigeration technology we can enjoy the taste of summer strawberries when snow is lying on the ground, or bite into a mango, which is as juicy and fresh as when it was picked, 3000 miles away.

But is this necessarily a good thing?

Most good chefs, for instance, abhor cooking with foodstuffs that are out of season, because frozen foods lack the texture and taste of fresh, and tinned or dried foods are, in haute cuisine terms, a non-starter. They want vegetables that are straight out of the soil and fish that was bought at the harbour that very morning. In short, they want it seasonal and will go so far as to tailor their menus to suit.

As well as tasting better, seasonal food is higher in nutrients. If you consider that a vegetable begins to lose nutrients as soon as it is harvested, then naturally the sooner it is on the table the better. If it has a lengthy plane journey ahead or a year to steep in sauce, then it is going to be all the poorer for it.

When shopping for fresh produce, choose items that are grown locally, is possible. The nearer its country of origin, the less distance it has had to travel. If you must buy preserved produce, choose frozen as it retains more vitamins than food preserved by any other method.

Choosing organic produce is an even better idea. Organic food is grown without recourse to the pesticides and hormones used to ensure that, for example, carrots are bright orange and have regular shape, and that dairy cows produce sufficient quantities of milk. The stuff you find in the organic range may be less aesthetically pleasing, but in terms of health benefits, it wins by a clear head. Eating organically, you will instantly decrease the amount of toxins you ingest because, no matter who how well processed, most non-organic foods contain chemical residues.

Supermarkets are increasingly responding to consumer demand by stocking wider ranges of organic produce although it still remains relatively expensive. However, as more and more people buy it, the price will naturally decrease.

Another way to ensure that your fruit and vegetables, milk, cheese, eggs, meat (and even wine) are organic, locally produced and bang on season is to subscribe to a local organic box scheme. For as little as five or six pounds, you can have a boxful of fresh produce delivered to your door from a local grower. Contact the Soil Association (www.soilassociation.org.uk) for details of schemes in your area.

Interestingly enough, many people who adopt a healthier lifestyle also adopt a healthier respect for the world around them, leading them towards fairly traded and organically grown foodstuffs. Yoga practitioners put this down to an increase in self-respect – the more you value yourself, the more inclined you are to value other people and other things.

3 Write it all down

One of the best ways to keep a good habit going is to keep a diary. It won't win the Booker Prize, but it will help you stay on track.

Buy a book especially for the purpose, rather than just scribbling your thoughts on a bit of paper while promising yourself to transcribe them into a book some time in the future – you won't. And try to make an entry for every day.

Describe how you feel, both physically and emotionally, note what you eat, what exercise you've done, even if it was just a case of using the stairs instead of the lift. Every little bit counts, so write it all down. If you are feeling discouraged, pour it all out, using the diary as your outlet rather than resorting to the fish and chip shop.

Not only is this exercise very therapeutic, it will

help you stay motivated. Do you really want to have to enter that you smoked five cigarettes, downed three gin and tonics and ate a take-away curry?

Many successful slimming clubs advocate weekly meetings and food diaries for exactly this reason. When you know you have someone or something to explain yourself to, it is amazing how strong-willed you can become.

A diary will also keep you focussed. Why are you doing this? And for whom? If your aim is to be trim and full of vitality for your summer holiday, remind yourself in words. Pen a little future fantasy involving a good-looking you, a white beach and a lot of blue sky.

A written record shows you how far you've come. Those first days of munching through salads will seem a long way off when you are choosing fruit over chocolate *because you prefer it*, your clothes fit better and your skin is so clear, it glows.

When you're feeling uninspired, re-read your story so far – better than any bestseller, guaranteed.

4 Get moving

If you seriously want to get healthy, you'll have to get moving. The good news for those who haven't been running since they left school is that getting physically fit doesn't require expensive gym membership or lung-busting slogs up steep hills at six o'clock in the morning.

In fact, if you and exercise have become a stranger,

you will do yourself more harm than good if you throw yourself in at the deep end.

Begin by walking. Getting off the bus two stops early and using the stairs instead of the lifts is good stuff. Your aim is to raise your heart rate a little, get yourself slightly out of breath and get your muscles attuned to the idea that they are going back to work after the long holidays.

Aim for a few minutes every other day to begin with, building up to, for instance, three 20-minute walks a week.

If you have any heart or respiratory problems, consult your doctor before embarking on any exercise programme. He or she will be able to outline how to go about it, or refer you to someone who can.

If you are reasonably fit but cannot seem to get any kind of fitness programme together, consider making a chart of what you want to achieve throughout a week. Build up your exercise levels gradually, including both high-impact (running) and low-impact (cycling or swimming) cardio-vascular work, as well as stretching (Pilates, yoga, or just a series of stretches you can do at home) and toning, ideally with weights.

A comprehensive seven-day fitness plan is contained later in the book.

If you are not good at self-motivation, seek expert advice from a gym instructor, who will be more than happy to create a personal fitness plan.

Or, even more glamorously, hire a personal trainer.

To cut costs, hire one between two or three of your friends. The trainer won't object and you will all benefit from such a one-to-one service.

Fit people aim to exercise for about three hours a week. But don't stop at that. The more active you are, the greater your general fitness. So get up from your desk and walk around. Take three minutes to have a really good upper body stretch. Walk all the way to work if it's fine weather. Go on!

5 Allergies

Food intolerances or food allergies, alongside Prada handbags and personal trainers, have become a very trendy thing to have. And it is hard not to think that, with all these famous people claiming gluten and dairy allergies, surely a fair proportion of us must have them too?

Well in fact, probably not.

Recent research found that very few of us have allergies to food, which is not to say that, when they are present, they are not extremely serious.

If you suspect a food allergy, you should contact your GP and have it investigated properly rather than attempt a serious of elimination diets that prove nothing and leave you listless and undernourished.

The most commonly cited food suspects are milk, eggs, wheat and gluten, shellfish and additives, with symptoms including digestive upsets (constipation, diarrhoea, bloating), skin sensitivity, migraine and even asthma.

However, these symptoms may be caused by other problems, so it is essential that you consult a doctor. He or she can refer you to a dietician who can help you discover if you are suffering from a food allergy and what to do about it.

If you have a suspected nut allergy, or any other known serious reaction to a particular food or substance, you should eliminate it from your diet immediately and consult your doctor as this can trigger potentially fatal anaphylactic shock.

6 Stress

Everyone experiences stress. Without it we would be so laid back we would hardly move, our lives would be at a standstill and we'd be incapable of reacting to danger (for example, jumping out of the way of a car that looks like it means to mow you down).

Stress, in physiological terms, means the release of adrenalin into the bloodstream caused by panic or fear. Known as the 'flight or fight syndrome', this flood of adrenaline enables athletes to break world records, soldiers to fight for their lives in battlegrounds, and helped our ancestors flee from the jaws of sabre-toothed tigers.

It is an excellent little bit of biology as it ensures that the body is focussed on crucial areas – the leg muscles needed for running, the arm and back muscles for fighting. Meanwhile the rest – the digestive system, for instance – goes on a temporary go-slow. Physical activity uses up the adrenaline, and the body returns to normal.

However, this ancient red alert system continues to function even in circumstances where it isn't needed. For instance, in a crowded noisy office while you're trying to finish an important report, or during a petrifying presentation in front of your most important clients.

What are you going to do with all the adrenaline? Run for your life?

Yet without a physical outlet that adrenaline will stay in your bloodstream, diverting blood from your digestive tract and pushing up your heart rate and blood pressure, making you sweat more and your mouth go dry.

Needless to say, your natural toxin elimination processes go straight out the window. Therefore, if you ate a heavy lunch and polished it off with a double espresso and a can of cola just before your body hit the stress button, you are going to be living with that lunch for some time to come.

And what has all this got to do with detoxing?

In short, if you are to have a hope of detoxing your system, you are going to have to manage your stress levels or it simply will not work.

By far the best way, far better than essential oils in the bath and a massage and facial at the weekend, is regular exercise. Even when you are frazzled by

work, a two mile cycle or a quick run round the block
will do wonders.

Not only will it draw a clear dividing line between
work and home life and enable you to sleep better
afterwards, it will clear your system of adrenaline
and allow it to revert to normal. Your heart rate will
go back to its resting rate, your blood pressure will
drop and you will sweat less.

And your body will be able to benefit from that delicious
wholefood meal you're going to rustle up for it.

7 Side effects

If you have ever suffered from a hangover you will
understand that detoxing is not without side effects.
The morning after the night before finds your liver
in a state of high industry. As it battles to expel its
sudden burden of toxins, your body starts to show
symptoms of this rapid detoxification process in the
form of a coated tongue, a raging thirst, nausea, not
to mention headaches, exhaustion and irritability.

A detox diet can produce something similar in the
side effects line but it won't last long and it is a sign
that your efforts are paying off – even if it doesn't
always feel like it!

The more 'toxic' you are, the more severe the
symptoms will be so if, for instance, you begin a detox
programme after a long festive season of rich food,
heavy drinking and smoky parties, brace yourself for
some tough symptoms.

You may initially feel very tired and, if you can, you should take a 20-minute nap when you feel you need it. You may also fall prey to the dreaded furry tongue and have a bit of bad breath. Brushing your teeth, and your tongue, can help to contain these symptoms, as can chewing a little parsley, which is renowned for its odour-neutralizing properties.

Headaches are common in the first few days, particularly if you are used to drinking a lot of tea and coffee. Drink plenty of water as this will help to flush out the toxins that little bit faster – taking your headaches with them.

Constipation and diarrhoea may occur which seems odd given that the diet is designed to regulate the body's excretory functions. Don't worry. This is quite common and your symptoms will disappear shortly. If they persist, see your doctor just in case there is an underlying health problem of which you may have been unaware.

Irritability is quite likely, which is why so many people choose to have their first couple of detox days to themselves. This is not always possible of course, so warn your nearest and dearest and don't commit yourself to anything anxiety-inducing, such as stressful family gatherings or extended baby-sitting duties! Be selfish and buy yourself some peace and quiet.

Taking a brisk walk or having a long soak in a lavender-scented bath are great for calming the nerves.

These side effects are unpleasant but try not to let

them put you off. Remember – what is happening is that the toxins you have accumulated over the last few months are finally being released from your fat cells in order to be processed and, finally, eliminated.

One of these days you are going to wake up feeling lighter and fresher than you have in years, so hold on tight.

Go!

The initial detox diet is a seven-day plan, ideally beginning on a Saturday so that you have two days at your leisure to adjust to the new regime.

Once the seven-day period is complete, you can adapt the diet to suit you in the long term or, if you eat a fairly good balance of nutrients anyway, you may revert to normal, with the odd tweak here and there, such as the elimination of coffee or added salt.

The Weekend Refresher is designed to 'top up' your levels of energy and is ideal for coming down after a period of indulgence.

Detox Foods

The chances are that if you've read this far you are already convinced you want to detox and are probably raring to get started. But, before you begin, there are a few things to consider

Knowing when the time is right

As mentioned in the previous chapter, the best time to begin is when you have at least a couple of days of leisure so you can adjust to your new lifestyle.

... And when it isn't

A period of intense stress at work, when deadlines are tight and there is pressure from all sides, is not a good time to turn your dietary world upside down.

For the first week it is also a good idea to avoid any social engagement that involves a drinking or eating situation. Even if you do stick to still mineral water and a green salad, the smoky, noisy atmosphere of a pub or restaurant will leave you feeling far from fresh and detoxed.

If you have recently suffered a bout of 'flu or any other kind of illness, give yourself a couple of weeks to recover before embarking on a detox plan. Your body is below par – the last thing it needs is more disruption.

If you are on prescription drugs, wait until the course is finished as they can interfere with the process of detoxification.

If you are pregnant or breastfeeding, consult your GP before making any dietary changes and always err on the side of caution. Having a baby takes a huge toll on your body and, while the benefits of detox are great, the process of change can be quite hard going.

Those in recovery from alcohol or drug addiction should also be cautious and wait until their bodies are stronger.

Before you begin

Book yourself a treat for the end of the first week. Think of something that rewards your body, but isn't food, as it is good to break the link between gratification and eating. Consider a luxurious massage, something new to wear or a day out by the sea.

While engaged in your detox routine, try to make mealtimes special. If you habitually wolf down your food in front of the television or while reading a book, you will miss out on taste and texture, and wind up feeling dissatisfied and wanting to eat more.

Instead, set the table and sit down to eat, without interruption and with a minimum of ambient noise. That way, you'll make the most of your food *and* be able to think about what you are eating, and why. The more mental reinforcement of the programme there is, the better. That way you stick with it and, according to some psychological research, the more you think about becoming fitter and healthier, the fitter and healthier you will become.

Make sure you have got your meal plans organized, your shopping done and your goal firmly in your mind.

And off you go.

Good foods, great foods and superfoods

There is no such thing as a bad food. Some foods are better than others and, for now, you are going with the good ones. Below is a list of the best detox foods, with a little explanation of why they are on the recommended list.

Good foods

Bananas: the ideal snack, they come with their own wrapping and are rich in potassium, which helps to regulate blood pressure. Also perfect as a pre and post work-out food as they contain natural sugar that is released quickly into the bloodstream.

Chickpeas: high in protein and therefore a healthy alternative to meat. However, they should be eaten in combination with vegetables and wholegrains such as rice or bread in order to provide the body with essential amino acids.

Courgettes: taste as good raw as cooked and are therefore very versatile. They are rich in beta-carotene and vitamin C and provide fibre. Courgette flowers make an exciting addition to salads and starters.

Honey: spoonful for spoonful, honey is actually sweeter than sugar. It is known as a good decongestant, a very mild laxative and stimulates the production of endorphins, the body's natural painkillers.

Lentils: high in protein and soluble fibre, which helps to lower blood cholesterol, and insoluble fibre, which helps to prevent constipation and lowers the risk of colonic cancer.

Nut butters, excepting peanut butter, which is very high in fat: try cashew nut or hazelnut butter for a change, preferably without added salt.

Meat: choose fresh cuts of lean meat rather than meat products such as sausages, which are packed with cereals and preservatives. Give meats like salami and bacon a miss too.

Pumpkin seeds: delicious roasted, and rich in potassium, magnesium and zinc. If you smoke or are trying to quit, chances are you will be slightly deficient in zinc, so ensure your diet includes it. Also a good, natural source of iron.

Sunflower seeds: like pumpkin seeds, they are full of flavour and minerals, including vitamin E, which is good for the skin.

Tofu: hugely versatile and absorbs the flavours in which it is cooked. It is high in protein and vitamin E and low in saturated fat, so long as you avoid frying it. However, it is often cited as a food allergen so, if you have never eaten it before, start small and see how you get on.

Wholemeal flour and products thereof: including wholewheat pasta which, once you're used to it, is a great deal tastier than the traditional bleached variety. And also much better for your liver.

Great foods
Aubergines: once thought to induce bad breath and madness, this glossy Indian vegetable provides lots

of fibre for very few calories – so long as you don't fry it. Because of its absorbent nature a 100g portion can soak up to 300 calories worth of oil.

Avocados: a popular ingredient in facial masks, avocados are a great source of vitamin E and antioxidants, which both promote healthy skin.

Barley: good source of fibre.

Buckwheat: good source of fibre.

Butter: include it because all diets must contain some fat – ideally at a ratio of less than 35% but more than 30%. Choose unsalted, organic varieties and avoid eating butter that has become discoloured, as this means it is turning rancid.

Chicken: choose free range and organic, not only because it is more ethical but also because the meat will be purer and less riddled with chemicals designed to artificially stimulate growth.

Eggs: go for free range and organic. Take care to read the labels because organic does not always mean free range and vice versa. You want both. Note too that if the box says 'Farm Fresh' but not 'Free Range', then the eggs are not free range. Eggs are essential to your diet as they contain protein, lecithin and vitamin B_{12}, which you need for a healthy nervous system, particularly if you are a vegetarian.

Goat's and sheep's cheese: easier to digest than regular cow's milk cheeses. They are also a great option for people who have developed an intolerance to cow's milk.

Millet: gluten-free, and a useful cereal for people with a gluten intolerance. Can be used to make Asian flat breads.

Peppers: delicious eaten raw in salads and a good source of vitamin C, beta-carotene and bioflavinoids, making them an ideal antidote to free radical damage.

Porridge: It is not only very warming and filling but a good source of soluble fibre, which can help to reduce cholesterol levels.

Potatoes: versatile, full of vitamin C, fibre, starch and potassium, cheap and easy to cook. Choose organic if possible and retain as much of the skin as you can – that's where all the goodness is.

Soya milk and soya milk products: they make a good alternative to cow's milk products and are easier to digest as they don't contain lactose, the natural sugar found in milk.

Superfoods

Apples: full of pectin, a soluble fibre that helps lower blood cholesterol and prevent constipation.

Artichokes: renowned for their detoxification properties.

Bean shoots: because they are new plants, they are packed with vitamins designed to sustain the new growth. When a bean starts shooting, its vitamin C content increases several hundred times. They make a crunchy, super-fresh addition to any salad.

Beetroot: this vivid pink root is a highly concentrated cocktail of vitamins and minerals, and is recommended as an anti-carcinogen and for combating cystitis. It is also rich in folate, which is essential for cell growth and is therefore recommended for pregnant women and those hoping to conceive. In terms of detoxing, it is believed that beetroot helps to increase the amount of bile secreted by the liver, thus making the excretion of waste from the body more efficient.

Brown rice: much tastier than the white variety and a great aid to your liver because it collects toxins as it moves through your gut and flushes them out. Short grain rice is best as it is the most absorbent.

Cabbage: renowned for its detoxification properties. The cabbage family includes turnip and brussels sprouts, which should all be cooked lightly for maximum vitamin retention. Brussels sprouts, possibly the most unpopular vegetable of all time, can be used to make a deliciously crunchy coleslaw – just wash, chop up finely and coat with mayonnaise.

Carrots: high in vitamin C and beta-carotene, and the basis for a wonderful variety of soups and fresh juices.

Citrus fruits: oranges, grapefruits, limes and lemons are all high in vitamin C; lemon is also a good substitute for vinegar.

Cranberries: because they acidify urine, cranberries are extremely helpful for improving kidney function and are often prescribed for the relief of the symptoms of cystitis.

Dandelion root coffee: renowned as a liver tonic.

Fresh fish or, if you don't have a local fishmonger, frozen: if you must have tinned, choose fish in oil rather than brine, which is full of salt, and rinse well before eating. The so-called oily fish (mackerel, salmon, herring) contain omega-3 oils, which are vital for the development of eye and brain tissue and for protecting against cardiac and circulatory diseases. Aim for three portions a week.

Fresh ginger: much better than the powdered variety and a great aid to digestion. Ginger tea is also good, but read the label carefully as many mass-market herbal teas, packaged to look natural and pure, contain chemical preservatives and flavourings.

Fresh herbs: these can be bought from most supermarkets and will thrive on your windowsill.

Olive oil: you need fat in your diet to provide essential fatty acids. Olive oil is an unsaturated fat, meaning it can actually help to reduce blood cholesterol. Extra Virgin varieties are best.

Onions and garlic: both renowned for their detoxification properties and great for boosting the immune system. Can be added to all kinds of savoury dishes. If you cannot abide the taste or smell of garlic, odourless, easy to swallow capsules are available from most health shops and supermarkets.

Grapes: contain antioxidants that aid detoxification.

Lecithin: found in eggs and soy beans but can also be bought in granules and sprinkled over cereal or salads. It is an emulsifying agent that is known to improve the functioning of the liver and gallbladder. It is even rumoured to be a good cure for cellulite though, sadly, the jury is out on that one!

Linseeds: can either be ground up and eaten for their fatty acids, which are regarded as very beneficent to liver function, or eaten as they are so that they provide a soft bulk in the intestines, designed to relieve constipation.

Peppermint tea: ideal for aiding digestion and a great pick-me-up if you're missing your caffeine kick start.

Radishes: rich in vitamin C and possessed of natural diuretic qualities.

Rice cakes: a great alternative to bread.

Slippery elm powder: the powdered inner bark of the elm tree and available from health shops. Being a very gentle form of non-digestible carbohydrate it proceeds naturally through the gut, helping to flush toxins as it goes.

Spices: particularly turmeric, which is known to be good for your liver, whole nutmegs, which are ideal for flavouring both savoury and sweet dishes, and cinnamon, which makes a wonderful flavouring for apples.

Strawberries, raspberries and other soft fruits: there are berries for every season and they're all good. They contain bioflavinoids and vitamin C and are deemed delicious even by people who don't like fruit!

Watercress: full of beta-carotene, which is good for the liver. Great for soups and salads.

Foods to avoid

Alcohol: it takes your liver an hour to process a single unit when it could be tackling your backlog of toxins instead. Even though red wine is said to be rich in antioxidants, keep the bottle corked while you're detoxing.

Caffeine: a single cup of ground coffee contains as much as 115mg caffeine, making it a serious diuretic which is damaging to your detox in that it leads to dehydration. If you're a heavy coffee drinker, you may be in for a headache or two the first few days you go without. Make sure you drink plenty of water and the symptoms will soon pass.

Chocolate: though it may be the ideal 'mouth' food in that it melts on your tongue, it is high in sugars and fats and also contains caffeine.

Hydrogenated fats: examples include margarines, which are difficult to digest.

Mushrooms: though they are wonderful in terms of flavour, mushrooms can contain known carcinogenic substances such as hydrazines and nitrosamines, as well as accumulating toxic heavy metals like cadmium and lead.

Peanuts: contain a large amount of fat and starch.

Salt: try to wean yourself off salt, as many foods contain it anyway. You will find, after a day or two, that you can taste your food much better without it. Plus, it depletes your stocks of potassium and can cause water retention.

Smoked fish: can contain toxins.

Sugar: the world's greatest source of 'empty' calories contains no nutritional value whatsoever and disrupts blood sugar levels into the bargain. Read your food labels as many 'fat-reduced' dishes contain extra amounts of sugar.

Tomatoes: acidic and can upset digestion.

White flour, white bread, white rice, white pasta: these insulin-stimulating refined carbohydrates provoke the liver into secreting high levels of fat, which can lead to diabetes and heart disease.

Yeast and yeast extract: can cause a superfluity of *Candida albicans*, a yeast present in the gut responsible for the production of energy and vitamin K. Too much can cause thrush as well as more severe symptoms, including extreme fatigue, mood swings, irritable bowel syndrome (IBS) and joint pain. Sufferers are often prescribed a yeast-free diet and, because it is such a prevalent condition, yeast is generally excluded from detox diets, at least initially.

Helpful herbs

There are so many digestive herbs out there you could be forgiven for turning your nose up at them all. And truth be told, if your diet's good enough, you are hardly going to need them. But here is a quick guide anyway, just in case you fancy giving your detox a boost.

Black root: recommended for those suffering from constipation. As it is a natural laxative it should not leave you too dehydrated though you should use it sparingly.

Blue flag: known as a blood cleanser, is often prescribed for those suffering from skin problems due to a sluggish liver.

Cat's claw: usually prescribed as an immune system booster, it also helps destroy unhealthy gut bacteria.

Dandelion: renowned for its digestive properties, it works on the gall bladder, increasing the secretion of bile and thereby improving the body's ability to efficiently process food. It also reduces toxicity in the liver, water retention and high blood pressure and helps recover normal peristalsis, thus relieving constipation. For these many reasons, dandelion is strongly recommended as a detox-enhancing herb and is generally available in the form of dandelion coffee.

Kelp: often recommended as a hair supplement perhaps because hair, like skin, functions as a mirror to our inner health. This supplement helps to regulate metabolism, which is good if the detox diet is a radical departure from your regular eating habits. Kelp will help you avoid the 'slump' associated with a sudden change of diet.

Marshmallow root: recommended if your pre-detox diet was rich in junk foods. It contains mucilaginous compounds, which help to repair damage to the mucous membranes of the intestines, often caused by a diet of processed foods.

Milk thistle: this supplement has become extremely popular in the last few years, particularly as a hangover tonic. This is because it is known for its ability to reduce alcohol induced liver damage. For detox purposes, it improves liver function, protecting it from free radical damage and toxins and assisting regeneration. It can be bought to make into a tea but, as this is a fussy and pretty tasteless way to take it, most people prefer taking it in capsule form. One word of warning though, it's relatively expensive so buy in bulk whenever you see it on offer.

Turmeric: the spice you use to colour your curries is also a handy little detox herb. It stimulates the gallbladder's production of bile and is said to be helpful in combating liver disease.

Vervain: often prescribed for those suffering from anxiety or stress, making it the perfect detox aid for those who live with a lot of pressure. It protects the liver as it soothes the nerves.

Yellow dock: This is the one to use if you have skin problems associated with poor digestion and liver function.

Water

Drinking water is essential for a successful detox. Actually, water is essential for a successful life, so don't stint on it.

Around two-thirds of a human's body weight is water, which is continually being expelled and which therefore continually needs topped up. We lose about a third of a litre of water a day simply in the act of breathing, and the rest through sweating and excretion.

Although we obtain some water from food, we should drink around two litres a day as well. Most of us are lucky if we manage a third of that, as drinks such as tea and coffee don't count.

When you are on a detox, drinking water is particularly important, as you need it to flush out all those toxins. You may also find, as you drink more, that you have less headaches and are less prone to constipation. Even fluid retention, oft cited as a reason for not drinking adequate amounts of water, may be alleviated.

You may also find you have more energy as dehydration is one of the primary causes of lethargy, particularly in women. Sports coaches are often frustrated by the fact that, especially in this country, sports enthusiasts don't take the issue of hydration properly. Whereas in many other countries, competitors will stop regularly to top up their fluid levels, we tend to soldier on and our performances suffer.

So drink!

The good news it that you needn't shell out for expensive bottled water. Tap water is just as good for you. If you don't like the taste of your local water, cooling it in the fridge and adding a slice of lemon and a couple of cubes of ice can make a big difference.

However, one word of warning. If you notice bluish stains in your sink below the tap, this could be an indication of a high copper content in your water. Copper is very bad for you if absorbed in high doses and is associated with cirrhosis of the liver. Contact your local water authority if in doubt.

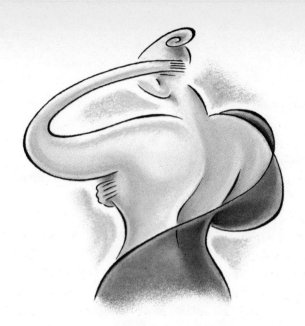

Towards the
Body Beautiful

A DETOX won't just make you feel good on the inside, it will make you look great on the outside. A healthy diet, strong on antioxidants and vitamins, works better than the most expensive skin cream on your complexion, better than any of those much-hyped, highly expensive cellulite pills on those areas where you've noticed a little sag or two, and much better than even a three week break at the most exclusive health farm in the world on your overall glow and poise.

And you want to help things along, now don't you?

Which is where dry-brushing, exfoliants and massages come into it. Missing these elements out won't sabotage your detox but including them will enable you to achieve maximum results.

Firstly, you must be regular in your habits. Scrubbing your face vigorously every once in a while will only upset its natural balance of oils and leave you with spots and dry patches. Far better to gently cleanse once a day and exfoliate twice a week in the bath, where the hot water will open your pores. Below are suggestions to help you establish a series of daily and weekly beauty routines to suit yourself.

Hair and scalp

Trichologists can look at your hair and work out exactly what's going on inside. If it's dull, brittle or prone to falling out, it means you are functioning below par. Your detox will go a long way to remedying that.

To give your scalp a boost, try performing this very basic yoga exercise every morning. Standing with your feet shoulders' width apart and your legs straight (but not locked at the knees), raise your arms above your head with your fingers outstretched. Now slowly bend at the hips – which are at the top of your legs, not at your waist, as we so often tend to think – keeping your arms straight, until your fingers touch your shins. You may even be able to touch the floor. Breathing slowly and deeply, hold for a count of ten, then straighten up slowly. Repeat once more.

This exercise causes the blood to flow towards your head, stimulating your scalp and promoting healthier, stronger hair growth.

Another way to give your scalp a little treat is to always give your hair a final rinse with cold water. This also closes the shafts of the hair, giving it a glossier look – ideal if you suffer from split ends. For added shine, cold rosemary tea used as a final rinse gives even the dullest hair a healthy sheen.

Face

Oceans of moisturizer won't do for your face what a little regular home massage will do.

In truth, the skin can absorb very little of what we slather onto it on a daily basis – the real moisture must come from within. To ensure this happens, you must keep your circulation in good condition, and gentle massage can help.

Do this when you are cleansing your face at night.

Having applied cleanser, line up your fingertips and gently press the skin of your forehead, working your way down to your eyebrows. Press down for around three to five seconds and then relax and move down.

When you reach your eye area, where the skin is very delicate, gently circle the eye sockets with your finger tips being careful not to drag the skin. Do this five times one way and five times the other, every single day. This is a great technique for combating and preventing bags under the eyes.

Now move to the cheeks, massaging the skin lightly with the fingertips in an outwards motion from the sides of the nose.

Continue down to the sides of the mouth, finally finishing by pressing along the skin of the jawbone.

Now that it's thoroughly rubbed in, remove your cleanser by applying a facecloth dipped in warm water. This gently opens your pores and helps extract residual grime and make-up.

Then splash your face several times with cold water till you feel your skin tightening up as the pores close again. This action also stimulates the skin, giving the circulation an extra boost.

Apply moisturizer sparingly, particularly around the eyes which, if over moisturized, often gain a puffy look – the very opposite of which you are trying to achieve.

Exfoliation is essential as it removes dead skin cells, leaving your complexion fresher and smoother. Choose a gentle facial scrub and use it regularly, ideally twice a week.

Face masks which double up as exfoliators are increasingly popular and a great idea as the mask draws out excess oils and accumulated dirt which can be then sloughed away along with the dead skin cells at the end.

Body

As you detox you will notice that the skin all over your body becomes softer of its own accord. This is because a healthy detox diet prevents your system becoming congested, a condition manifested in rough skin and poor circulation.

To maximize this, get into the habit of exfoliating the skin on your body on a regular basis. Some enthusiasts advocate daily skin scrubs but twice a week, so long as you keep at it, will do just as well.

Dry brushing, as advocated by Bridget Jones in her famous diary, is generally believed to be the best method of sloughing off dead cells. For this you need a clean brush composed of natural bristles.

Prior to a bath or shower, brush your skin in long sweeping motions, beginning with the soles of your feet and working up your shins, thighs, bottom and stomach, always working towards the heart. Don't forget arms and shoulders too, again working towards the heart.

Most people find dry brushing extremely uncomfortable at first but you do get used to it. Ensure that you don't brush too hard – the object of the exercise is not to bring your skin out in long red weals.

After your shower, apply a body moisturizer all over, paying particular attention to elbows, knees and ankles, where the skin is driest. The act of massaging in the moisturizer is great for boosting your circulation, so take your time and do it properly. Have a big glass of water afterwards as the skin loses moisture in baths and showers.

If dry brushing sets your nerves on edge, use a body scrub when you are in the bath or shower, again making sure you moisturize thoroughly afterwards.

A great home-made body scrub, which actually negates the need for moisturization, can be made by combining rough sea salt crystals with olive oil. Mix a ten pence-sized palmful of salt with a similar portion of oil and apply to skin directly. The roughness of the salt smooths the skin while the oil adheres to it leaving it beautifully silky. You can either pre-mix this, half and half, or keep a salt canister and olive oil bottle by the bath.

Unlike many body scrubs, it isn't perfumed, making it ideal for sensitive skins – and men!

Blissful bathtimes

Bathtime shouldn't be all work. There are many detox bath preparations on the market, mostly involving seaweed extract and designed to draw out poisons from the body. And they generally work, if only because the natural action of hot water and steam on the body does the job quite naturally.

Be careful not to make the water too hot, as this will dehydrate you unnecessarily. Aim for body temperature.

For maximum efficacy, do a series of deep breathing exercises while you are in your bath.

In fact, most of us breathe very shallowly, which means that we are not using our lungs to their full capacity and failing to inhale sufficient quantities of oxygen to keep our blood levels topped up. The result is a poor circulation, often manifesting itself as cold feet and hands, and poor skin tone.

Take a deep, deep breath now, so deep that the area beneath your ribcage expands, and feel how that inhalation affects your whole body, right down to your toes. If you feel yourself tingling, that's good – it's a sign that your circulation has been given a little oxygen boost.

The reason we breathe so shallowly is down to the way we live. When we're stressed, we breathe in short, shallow gasps and the habit spills over into non-stressed times. What makes us sigh at such times is a trigger from the body to make us take in more air.

When you are breathing deeply it is the area below your ribcage – the diaphragm – which should rise, not your chest. While lying in the bath, rest your hand on your diaphragm and practise breathing so that you can feel that area rising and falling with every breath.

Do ten breaths in all.

Not only will this ensure that you inhale all the lovely scents from your detox bath, it will speed up the elimination of toxins and slow down your heart rate. Which means that afterwards, you can look forward to a long, restful sleep.

Epsom Salts are recommended as a detox bath. They are available from most chemists and health food shops and are generally much cheaper than the designer label detox baths.

They are very rich in magnesium, though you will need at least 75g per bath to draw toxins from the body.

After your bath, which should not be more than 20 minutes long, keep yourself warm and don't plan on being able to complete any vigorous or mentally draining activity. Sleep is your best option.

And so to bed

Sleep is the best health and beauty treatment money can't buy and if you don't get enough of it, you'll age rapidly, your immune system will go downhill, your concentration and memory will be impaired and you will feel awful. Convinced?

The best kind of the sleep is the regular kind, be it eight or ten hours a night, so long as you retire and rise at approximately – that is, within a margin of 15 minutes – the same time every single day.

The traditional 'long lie' at weekends, when we mistakenly believe that a marathon sleep on Saturday and possibly also Sunday morning will pay back the body for a string of late nights, does you no good at all. In fact, if you have missed out on sleep, an extra hour or two the following night is all you need. Any more is a waste of time.

If your sleeping patterns are a bit wobbly, gradually work them into a regular pattern, adding to or subtracting from the morning or evening times in 15-minute blocks. You will eventually find that you can get to sleep at an appointed time and wake up feeling refreshed.

Sleep is essential for good health, particularly when you are subjecting yourself to a detox, because it is the one time when the body can attend to essential maintenance. This is when your cells are regenerated and tissues are repaired and why, following an accident or illness, your body craves hours and hours of extra sleep.

The regulation of your sleeping hours should iron out most sleep problems, but if you are still having trouble nodding off, here are a few tips:

Sleep in the dark
Your body is very light sensitive. It's a primordial sense, designed to make the human organism maximize its exposure to daylight and it means that, when there is light, the body thinks it should be waking up. Which is why we naturally waken early on bright summer mornings – and why we toss and turn when we leave the bedside light on. Studies have suggested that sleeping with the light on can impair a child's concentration the following day, so wean your kids off nightlights too.

Keep the bedroom uncluttered

Feng Shui dictates that bedrooms should be cool and clear. Not glory holes of soft toys and barely used furniture. The reasoning being that, if a room is busy, your mind will stay busy too. So give the room you sleep in a good clear-out, pare down the pictures and turn the bed so that you don't look through the door if possible – the outside world, even your humble hallway, will distract you from your slumbers.

Have a bath

When you emerge from a warm bath your body mimics exactly what it does when it goes to sleep. It cools downs and the heart rate reduces. Have one just before bed and you're already on the path to sleep. Note: a hot bath will only make you more restless.

Exercise

Don't exercise vigorously within two hours of trying to go to sleep, though a gentle night-time walk will help to soothe your nerves. Exercising earlier in the day will help you sleep, as it de-stresses you.

Sleep on your left hand side

This way the intestines are in the best position to do their work. Lying on your side with your head supported is the best position for your spine as lying on your front or back only accentuates the S-curve unnaturally, often causing backache.

The Seven-Day
Detox Plan

THIS seven-day plan is designed as a kick start to a healthy lifestyle rather than as a long-term strategy. If you are feeling loaded with toxins, it is tempting to consider an all-out fast but unless you are in superb health, this is hardly advisable. If you drink plenty of water you will find that you begin to flush out toxins quite rapidly anyway.

You may find that you feel more tired than usual to begin with. Go with it. Have a bath and an early night – your energy levels will return in due course. If you can, fit in a little exercise during the week too.

Eat as and when you are hungry and avoid sitting down to large meals. However, don't feel that you must go for long periods without food. You will probably lose a couple of pounds in weight anyway, simply because your diet is so high in raw fruit and vegetables, which is both filling and low in calories.

Make sure you include fish for essential protein and omega-3 oils, and olive oil for essential fatty acids. If you are concerned, take an additional multivitamin supplement, just to ensure your nutritional needs are covered. A cod liver oil supplement is also advisable.

You will find that your bowels move more often, in some cases up to three times a day. Unless this is accompanied by other symptoms, such as pain, diarrhoea or blood, there is nothing to worry about.

Ideally, choose a week when you are off work or your workload is light and start on Saturday. On waking every day, drink a cup of hot water with lemon juice. Hot water goes straight to the gut, stimulating it to begin working. It is also very good for clearing sinuses. Drink it half an hour before breakfast if you can manage the time so that your body has had a chance to wake up before you give it any nourishment.

NB: if you are allergic to any foods suggested below, miss them out completely. Your body won't cope any better simply because it is on a detox.

Week one

Foods to be avoided

The key word for this seven-day plan is cleansing. Your aim is, via dietary management, to help your liver work to its full potential. Which means eliminating any foods which might impair its performance.

Ordinary bread is therefore off the menu, though you can eat bread made without yeast, wheat, millet, oats, barley, rye or bran. Yeast is out because it may aggravate Candidiasis – the name for the condition caused by a superfluity of *Candida albicans* in the gut – while wheat and similar substances are often the root cause of food allergies, many of which are unsuspected.

Rice cakes make a surprisingly satisfying alternative.

Fermented dairy products, such as cheese and yoghurt, may also stimulate Candidiasis so they are excluded too. Choose soya or rice milk instead, ideally reinforced with calcium, a mineral that is just as essential for adults as it is for growing children.

Make sure you consume at least one egg every other day, and foods such as peas and lentils and seeds every day where possible, to compensate for lost nutrients.

Mushrooms are also off the menu, as are dried fruits and prepackaged fruit juices, though freshly squeezed is fine.

By avoiding these foods and upping your intake of liver-friendly foods, the liver is able to produce more bile and thus regulate the level of *Candida albicans* in future.

Animal fats and vegetable fats such as coconut and palm oil are out because they make extra work for the liver. Choose olive oil or good quality sunflower oil instead.

Sugar, alcohol, caffeine and salt are also banned this week.

Foods to be enjoyed

If the staples of your diet are bread and butter and tea – and it is surprising how many people this applies to – the above list may make for devastating reading.

However, there is a lot of healthy food out there, and you'll be surprised at the variety on offer, even on this relatively severe detox week.

Fruit is, of course, more than welcome. Ideally, get it fresh and in season, though tinned fruit in fruit juice is a reasonable alternative where this isn't possible.

If you are not much of a fruit-eater, buy a juicer and start making your own juice drinks.

Vegetables are also good. Aim for two or three generous portions of green leafy stuff a day whilst keeping root vegetables such as potatoes restricted to a more modest single daily portion.

Pulses and dried beans are a great source of protein and should be eaten regularly. If you are not used to them you may find them quite difficult to digest at first. Start with small portions first, making sure that you chew properly and that your beans are properly cooked. Such precautions should guard against the dreaded wind problem!

Sunflower and olive oil are good in small quantities, and provide a basis for excellent stir-fries.

Nuts such as brazil nuts, cashews and almonds are delicious and very nutritious, but also high in fat, so don't go crazy. A handful a day is sufficient. Sunflower and pumpkin seeds are also recommended.

Poultry is fine for this week, so long as it is lean, unsmoked and you refrain from blackening it under the grill. Choose organic and free range if at all possible as this ensures the meat is truly untainted.

Unsmoked, fresh fish is another healthy option, although the skin, which is very fatty, should be removed. Your fishmonger will do this for you.

Brown rice, as mentioned in the previous chapter, is a great cleanser so do include this in your seven-day plan. Puffed rice is an excellent breakfast option.

And don't forget those eggs.

Juices
One of the best aids in a detox plan is a juicer. With

one of these little gadgets to hand you can make yourself a vitamin-packed drink in no time.

It also means you can make a handful of fruit and vegetables more palatable without having to cook it – a process that inevitably leads to at least a little nutritional loss – or slathering it in salt or sugar.

Even when you're not on a detox, home-made juice is a great way to ensure you eat your World Health Organization requirement of five fruit or vegetables portions per day. Particularly if you prove resistant to the habit of munching apples and celery throughout the day.

However, if you are not used to eating large amounts of fruit and vegetables, don't go mad with the juices to begin with. Bloating and wind are great disincentives when you are trying to change your habits for the better.

One home-made juice a day is enough, with a couple of portions of vegetables later on, and another small portion of fruit.

Carrots, apples and cooked but not pickled beetroot work well together, as do oranges with a dash of lemon.

To prepare, simply wash as usual, peeling where necessary, cut into largish chunks and throw into the juicer.

Further ideas are contained in the recipes section.

Meal suggestions followed by an asterisk (*) are featured in the recipes section.

Breakfast ideas

Puffed rice (the sugar-free variety) with a sprinkle of pumpkin seeds, a chopped apple and rice or soya milk

A boiled egg served with rice cakes

Ginger Scrambled Eggs*

Home-made Muesli*

Lunch and snack ideas

Home-made hummus served with crudités*

Carrot, Honey and Ginger Soup*

Parsnip and Apple Soup*

Express Lentil Soup*

Jacket potato with tuna (tinned in brine and well-drained) and salad

Rice Salad
(composed of a portion of brown rice cooked with a dash of bouillon to give it added flavour, chopped peppers and onions and a handful of unsalted cashew nuts)

Stir-fried Beansprouts*

Broccoli with Almonds*

Main meal ideas

Cashew Nut Risotto*

Potato Omelette with Herbs*

Spicy Lentil Dhal*

Vegetable Hotpot*

Salad Nicoise*

Desserts
Apple Custard*
Banana and Almond Cream*
Baked Pears*

A typical day's detox

On rising

On rising drink some hot water and lemon juice. Take advantage of an empty stomach to perform some simple stretching exercises. These will help get your blood pumping and your skin glowing.

Begin with the stretch outlined in the hair and scalp section in the previous chapter.

The triangle

Next, move your feet so that they are three to four feet apart with your right foot pointing to the right and your left foot pointing forwards. Raise your arms so that they form a straight line parallel to the floor.

Take a deep inward breath and, as you exhale, stretch your right hand down to your right ankle so that your left arm, still in line with the right, points towards the ceiling.

Turn your head so that you are looking up at your left hand and hold that stretch for a count of five.

Raise yourself upright and repeat for the other side.

This gives your spine a good stretch.

Now stand with your feet together, your arms straight in front of you and your fingers interlocked.

Step your right foot back two feet or so and, keeping your left leg bent and your right leg straight, stretch, flexing your arms as you go.

Repeat for the other side.

This is excellent for stretching your calf muscles and your arms.

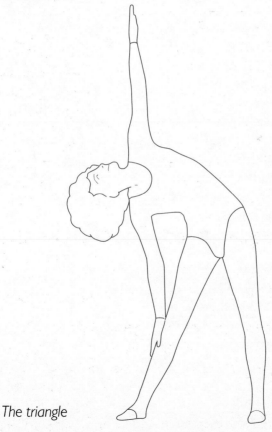

The triangle

Hamstring stretch
Now, with feet together again, lift your right knee up, using your arms, to your chest. Repeat for the other side, five times each side.

This gives your thighs and hamstrings a stretch.

The mountain
Finally, stand erect with your arms by your sides and imagine your head is attached to the ceiling by an invisible thread. Breathe deeply in and out and enjoy this most basic and beautiful of yoga poses – called the Mountain posture.

Take a moment to think about why you are detoxing and what you aim to achieve by doing it.

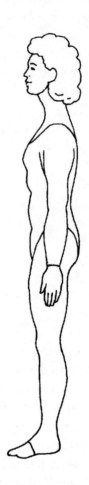

The mountain

Breakfast
A boiled egg served with rice-cakes

Mid-morning
Make up some hummus and serve with salad or rice cakes – or both.

Remember, this is not a weight loss diet so don't feel you have to skimp on portions. Eat as much as you want and enjoy what you eat.

Lunch
Home-made carrot, honey and ginger soup. Follow with an apple or pear or a handful of berries.

Mid-afternoon
Have a dandelion coffee or a mint tea. If you're hungry, have a couple of rice cakes or a handful of seeds and nuts.

Make sure you are drinking plenty of water and don't be alarmed if you feel a little bloated. The combination of the fibre contained in the vegetables and the increase in your water intake may make you feel this way. Don't drink so much water that you feel water-logged and unwell.

An hour after your mid-afternoon snack is an ideal time to put in some aerobic exercise, particularly as this usually coincides with the end of the working day.

Why not power walk for 15 minutes? Or put in 20 minutes on the exercise bike?

If you are self-conscious, wait till you get home, put on a record with a fast beat and dance vigorously for 20 minutes instead. Exercise doesn't have to be dreary and repetitive to be effective.

Afterwards, have a quick shower to give your circulation a boost and don't forget to drink some water to top up your hydration levels.

Dinner
White fish ratatouille with brown rice. Chop up a courgette, pepper and onion, and lightly sauté in a generous tablespoonful of olive oil. Serve this with your poached or grilled fillet of white fish and a portion of brown rice.

Evening snack
A cup of warming ginger tea plus a small handful of brazil nuts which are rich in selenium, believed to be effective in combating low moods.

Soak for 20 minutes in a detox bath and then retire to bed. You've earned it.

This is just an example of how a typical detox day might go if you are following a strict seven-day plan.

When the week is up you will notice a profound change in your skin tone and energy levels, your bowel movements will be more regular and you may well have lost a pound or two.

Try to avoid celebrating with a slap-up dinner and a night in the pub.

Have a healthy meal instead and award yourself no more than two glasses of red wine. A detox won't have a lasting effect if you immediately resume all your bad habits.

Longer-term detoxing

Having discovered that detoxing is not such a trial after all, and that the benefits are worth their weight in beetroot, what next?

The harsh truth is that, if you immediately resume all your bad habits, you will very soon resume all your niggling health and fitness problems.

Then again, staying on the severe seven-day detox forever is not going to do you any favours either – in fact, such a restricted diet could do your health irreparable damage.

The solution is to gradually reintroduce various foods into your diet as the weeks progress, while sticking with the important habits.

Important habits
*Keep up the water intake – 2.5 litres a day
*Five portions of fresh fruit and vegetables a day, every day
*Eat when hungry, and not before
* No coffee, no cola, no tea, no hot chocolate
* Omega-3 oils three times a week
* Low to zero alcohol

* No added salt
* No added sugar

Assuming you have completed the seven-day detox, what follows is a run-down of the next few weeks.

Weeks two and three

Foods to be enjoyed
As before, only now you can also include millet, barley and rye – making bread an option, though choose a yeast-free variety. You can also eat rye biscuits and pasta made from rye flour. Stay off the wheat and corn a week or two longer.

Buckwheat is a good option, and very filling.

Porridge oats, which make a very filling and cleansing breakfast.

Yoghurt and cheese, though stick to goat's and sheep's milk varieties.

Breakfast ideas
Muesli

(quarter pint of rice or soya milk and three tablespoonfuls of millet flakes. Leave to soak for ten minutes. Mix in a small handful of sunflower seeds, a small handful of pumpkin seeds and a chopped apple or pear. Top with natural yoghurt.)

Porridge with stewed apples or honey
Fresh natural yoghurt served with a chopped
up apple or pear and a sprinkling of pumpkin seeds
Yoghurt Shake
(made with chopped fresh fruit, a portion
of fresh yoghurt and a handful of ice cubes
– mixed into a smoothie in the liquidizer.)

Main meal ideas
Buckwheat Bake*
Tomato and Bean Stew*
Nut Loaf*
Stuffed Peppers*
Goat's cheese salad
(with rice cakes, green leaves, and fresh
basil. For an extra touch, toast the cheese
lightly under the grill before serving.)
Braised Barley with Vegetables*
Desserts
Banana Crumble*
Yoghurt Ice Cream*

Weeks four and five

Foods to be enjoyed
As before, only now you can also include wheat and
corn. If, however, this addition doesn't feel so good,

now is the time to see your GP and discuss the issue of food allergies.

Remember, just because you crave a food, it does not mean it is necessarily good for you. Think of all the people who crave strong alcohol!

Keep yeast off the menu for Week Four but allow it in during Week Five. Again, watch out for side effects. As this will mean a return to bread, try to stick to wholemeal varieties at all times. You've come so far – why start backsliding now?

Mushrooms are also back, and a little dried fruit if you fancy.

Cow's milk can also make a return, though stick to semi-skimmed where possible. You could also make (very) sparing use of unsalted, organic butter.

Organic red meat can also come back on board.

Breakfast ideas
Easy Kedgeree*
Healthy Hash Browns*
Cornmeal Muffins*

Main meals
White Fish Terrine*
Mushroom and Cashew Nut Stroganoff*
Wholewheat Penne with Pesto and Cherry
    Tomatoes*
Lamb with Rosemary*

The Weekend Refresher

ATWO-DAY detox is not going to transform your life. You won't go home on Friday feeling fat, lethargic and tired of life and re-emerge on Monday morning looking and feeling like a supermodel. If only.

But you will have a spring in your step and you will look and feel better. You will also benefit from the selfish aspect of this plan.

Most of us – particularly women – rarely take time out for ourselves. Even when we've planned a treat, it is usually for the family, our partner, or our friends.

Detox

This time it is all about you. So capitalize on this and make it a full-blown luxury weekend for yourself – without the crippling expense of booking into a residential spa.

First up, clear your schedule. Don't take any work home, don't arrange to go out on Saturday night, don't even *think* about cleaning the bathroom or painting the back bedroom.

If you are married with children, persuade your spouse to take them away for the day or, even better, the whole weekend.

Then again, if you are due a haircut or beauty treatment and you know it will be a pleasurable experience, go right ahead and book.

Jane Clarke, in her book *Bodyfoods for Women*, suggests buying up a stock of your favourite magazines and a couple of books by your favourite authors. Add a few beauty products you've been meaning to try out and you have all you will need by way of entertainment.

She also advises that you stock up well on fresh fruit and vegetables, fresh herbs and plenty of lemons and limes, which are great for spicing up drinks and dressing salads.

Once your food cupboard and fridge are bristling with newly plucked greenery, you are all set to go.

Just don't forget to switch the phone over to the answering machine.

Friday night

You have just slammed the door on another hectic week and what wouldn't you give for a large gin and tonic and a cigarette? Sorry, but if you give in to that urge, your weekend detox is already at an end.

Too many drinks, combined with a take-away and a late night and your weekend will be taken up recovering. Heavy drinking takes an especially long time to recover from because, no matter what you do, your body cannot process more than one unit (that is, half a pint of lager or a small glass of wine) per hour.

Athletes are generally advised that it takes at least three days before they return to full fitness after even moderate drinking so just think what a round of vodka and cokes will do for your health plans.

In Britain we work the longest hours in Europe yet our status as employees is amongst the lowest in the Western world. Therefore it is hardly surprising that we suffer tremendous amounts of work-related stress, which spills over into unhealthy alcohol intake, smoking, lack of exercise and poor sleeping habits.

Which results in an increased incidence of tiredness, hangovers and lack of energy which, in turn, makes us more inclined than ever to drink/smoke/lie awake half the night worrying.

It is a strong person indeed who can manage a stressful, perhaps unsatisfying job and suffer no depletion to their health.

All this aside, promise yourself that this weekend,

no matter how many times your boss yelled at your unnecessarily or how grim next week looks like being, you are going to break the stress-binge cycle.

As soon as you get home, get changed.

Stepping out of your work clothes and into something loose-fitting and comfortable provides an important psychological demarcation between the day and the evening. By changing into your own clothes, perhaps taking off your make-up and jewellery too, you are signalling to yourself that you are now in your own time.

If you still feel like you are wired to the moon, and most of us do, step into a quiet room, preferably an uncluttered one, light a candle and prepare to do a ten-minute yoga routine.

Ten-minute yoga

Begin by placing a mat on the floor. You can buy dedicated yoga mats quite cheaply from sports supply shops. Or you can improvise using a sturdy blanket folded over on itself. If you have bare wooden floorboards in your room, perhaps use two blankets – the object of the exercise is to protect the bones of your spine when you lie down and your knees when you kneel.

1. The thunderbolt

To start, kneel so that your bottom is resting on your heels and your back is very straight. Keep your head erect, as if it were connected to the ceiling by an invisible string and allow your shoulders to relax without sagging.

Rest your hands, palms upwards, in your lap.

As soon as you are comfortable, close your eyes and take a deep inward breath, so that you feel your diaphragm expand. Hold for a second and slowly breathe out, through your nostrils rather than your mouth.

Repeat ten times, slowly, while imagining that each inward breath is a column of pure white air and each outward breath is cloudy and grey with the toxins it is transporting out of your lungs.

After ten, open your eyes and, in your own time, stand up.

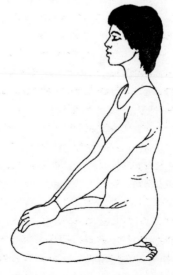

The thunderbolt

2. Half moon

With your feet shoulders' width apart and your arms by your sides, take a deep inward breath and, slowly, exhale.

Breathe in again and, this time, raise your arms above your head so that the tips of your fingers are touching and your upper arms are gently grazing your ears.

The half moon is a wonderful stretch for your back.

Take another deep breath and, on the exhale, bend to the right at the waist, maintaining the position of your arms. You will feel the stretch both in your back, your waist, and on your outer thigh.

Hold for as long as is comfortable and repeat for the other side, repeating the whole routine three times.

Now bend forward at

The half moon

the hips, again on the exhale, bringing your chest as close to your knees as you can. It is important to do the whole exercise very slowly – this is the secret of yoga. If you do it fast, that is when you pull muscles and tendons and generally end up feeling worse than you did when you started.

Hold for as long as is comfortable and then, on the exhale, raise yourself slowly upwards, taking care not to jerk your movements.

3. The warrior
Now let your arms hang by your sides, with your shoulders relaxed but not sloping, and your head erect. Place your feet three to four feet apart with the toes pointing forward.

Lift your arms so that they are straight and parallel

The warrior

to the floor and turn to face to the right. At the same time, point your right foot to the right and bend down on that knee until the right thigh is parallel to the floor and the right calf forming a right angle with it. Your left leg should be straight by now.

The warrior is said to be very empowering. It will give your thigh muscles a stretch, and help to tone up the muscles on your upper arms. Hold for a count of ten, or perhaps 20 if you can manage, before slowly and gently resuming the upright position.

Now repeat for the other side.

4. The cat
For the next stretch, kneel on all fours on the mat with your knees and hands shoulders' width apart and facing downwards, your head in alignment with your spine.

You will soon see why this is called the cat. Take a good deep breath and, on the exhale, arch your

The cat

back upwards without straining and without altering the position of your hands and knees. You should now be facing downwards as your head should be tucked into your chest, forming a continuous curve shape with your spine.

Return slowly to your central position. Take another deep breath and then do the reverse, making your spine describe a concave curve and with your head bending backwards so you face forward.

Return to normal and repeat twice.

5. The corpse

Finally, lie on your back with your head resting on the bony part at the back of your skull and your arms by your sides, your legs stretched out in front of you. If this isn't comfortable for your lower back, raise your knees so that your spine is level with the floor.

Take a series of deep breaths and allow your back

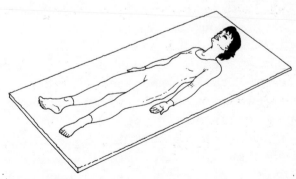

The corpse

to 'melt' into the floor, letting it feel heavy. According to practitioners of the Alexander Technique, you should perform this little back exercise for ten minutes every day. Why? Because gravity – in other words, standing up all day – is what makes our backs ache. It bears down on us, squashing the vertebrae together and causing back pain. Lying like this stretches the spine out, and allows the spinal fluid – the lubricating oil of the body – to trickle back into the vertebrae, allowing the back in turn to stretch out to its full potential.

A good ten minutes will achieve optimum results and, when you stand up again, you will find that a great deal of the tension in your lower back has vanished.

When you do get up, do it slowly, perhaps by rolling onto your side and raising yourself from there.

And you're done!

Friday food

By now you should be feeling a little more relaxed and the craving for stimulants should have reduced.

Capitalize on this with a drink of hot water with some freshly squeezed lemon juice. Warm drinks go straight to your gut, and help get everything moving again so think of this as the beginning of the end of all that junk you've been eating!

Drink it sitting down, perhaps listening to some music or just staring into space, letting your mind wander. It is incredible how rarely we simply 'stand

and stare' but, contrary to popular belief, it is actually very good for us.

Constantly working and thinking and ingesting information doesn't keep the brain active and bursting with vim. In fact, it does the opposite, stifling creativity and leaving us weary and unable to make mental connections. So give your brain a little detox too. Keep the TV off and just be with yourself for once.

As for your evening meal, your best bet is to dine early because, without caffeine or alcohol to keep you artificially stimulated, you will realize just how tired you really are at the end of the working week.

An ideal dinner is something easy to make and easy to digest – and full of the kinds of foods that get the detoxing process off to a flying start.

Why not make a pasta? No, not one of those rich, creamy pastas you eat in restaurants, but a healthy wholewheat pasta dish where the vegetables seriously outnumber the noodles.

Wholemeal pasta with fresh vegetables and pesto
Put 50g of wholewheat (not white!) pasta on to boil. While it cooks, chop up an organic onion and sauté it in olive oil until it becomes transparent.

Meanwhile, chop up a pepper, a handful of mangetout, a handful of baby corn, two tomatoes and a handful of unsalted cashews. Add them to the onion and sauté for two to three minutes. Drain your pasta and stir in a spoonful of organic pesto and serve.

Detox

Salad
Alternatively, make a large salad, with plenty of leaf, some roasted pumpkin or sunflower seeds and some grilled goat's cheese.

Soup
Or perhaps soup, which you could make in advance the night before. But don't pad it out with giant hunks of bread.

Snacks
If you are hungry later, restrict yourself to fresh fruit though, in all honesty, you probably won't be. Remember to drink at least two glasses of water during the evening and an extra one if you have a bath.

And so to bed
You should be in for a really good night's sleep, so make up the bed with fresh bedclothes, wear your finest pyjamas and enjoy.

Self-indulgent Saturday

On rising
Have a drink of hot water with lemon and follow up with a good stretch or perhaps a brisk ten-minute walk outdoors.

Breakfast
Choose a breakfast option from the seven-day detox menus.

The rest of the day is up to you!
The rest of the day is truly your own so why not use it to do something you never have a chance to do? Perhaps sitting in your favourite chair reading a novel undisturbed? When did you last do something like that? Or why not rent a couple of videos of your favourite films and prepare for a long day of self-indulgence?

If you want to do some exercise, by all means go ahead but don't feel that you need to.

Lunch and dinner
Choose lunch and dinner from the seven-day menu too, though don't leave it so long between meals that you feel weak with hunger. This isn't a weekend starvation programme. And prepare yourself a little treat too – perhaps some banana crumble or a large glass of freshly squeezed fruit juice. A portion of strawberries blended with a nectarine or peach makes a deliciously refreshing, summertime drink. In winter, blend carrots, an apple and an orange for a surprisingly tasty alternative which will also help stave off colds and flu thanks to its rich vitamin content.

Headaches
If you feel headachey, ensure that you are drinking

enough water – you are aiming for between two and three litres a day. Don't leave it till you feel thirsty as the body is a little like a car – it only sends out empty tank signals when it's really low in fuel.

You may suffer mild headaches if you are used to drinking a lot of tea and coffee. Go with it, substituting dandelion coffee for your usual cuppa. You'll feel better soon.

Fatigue

If you feel terribly sleepy, have a nap. However, try not to sleep for more than 20 minutes at a time during the day. You will find these cat-naps surprisingly refreshing but if you allow yourself to drift off for a couple of hours you will feel heavy and sleepy for the rest of the day.

Beauty treatments

Our continental cousins would faint if they knew how rarely we Brits go for facials. In countries like France and Spain it is just a regular part of life to step into the beauty salon twice a month for a facial. Over here, we make do with twice a year, regarding it as the ultimate self-indulgence. Consequently, beauty salons think they can charge us a fortune for the privilege.

But don't despair. You can give yourself a home facial for a fraction of the price and, even better, you know what skin products suit you.

NB: it is a better idea to have a facial on a Saturday rather than a Sunday as it can often bring blemishes to a head the following day.

A home facial
What you need:
A good facial cleanser
Cotton wool
A large bowl
A towel
A face-pack (recipes below)
Two used tea bags
A facial exfoliator
Eye cream
A good quality moisturizer

Begin by giving your face a good cleanse, to ensure you have removed any traces of old make-up and the residue from breathing urban air.

Half-fill a large bowl or basin with boiling water, adding half as much again of cold. You want lots of steam but not at the cost of scalding your face.

Now place your head over the bowl, using a towel to create a kind of tent around it. The steam should feel pleasantly warm. If it stings, it is too hot, so add more cold water immediately.

Stay in place for five to ten minutes, taking deep breaths. This won't just clear your sinuses, it will open your pores, making them easier to clean.

When you are done, pat your face dry and apply your face-pack, being careful to steer clear of the eye area which is very delicate.

Lie down on your bed or on your yoga mat, and place the two (cold!) used tea bags over your eyes. These will help to reduce any puffiness. They are also very refreshing if you feel at all headachey.

Once your face-pack has been in place for the requisite time, remove it using lukewarm water and a face-cloth. Don't scrub at your face – instead, place the wet cloth gently against the skin and let it lift the face-pack by itself.

When it is all removed, apply your facial exfoliator, scrubbing ever so gently in circular motions around the cheeks, forehead, mouth and neck area.

Wash away with lukewarm water.

To give your skin a moisture boost you can either buy a hydration mask or apply a thick, thick layer of your regular moisturizer. Once it is applied, relax for five minutes before rinsing gently.

Give your face a final splash all over with ice cold water. This will close the pores and give your cheeks a lovely rosy colour.

Apply a final, thin layer of moisturizer to your face and a thin layer of eye cream to the eye area.

NB: However logical it seems, applying heavy layers of moisturizer won't actually make your skin proportionately more moisturized. A thin layer applied when you need it is much more effective.

Face-pack recipes
Egg and almond face-pack
The egg whites tighten on the skin, which effectively gives your skin a bit of a 'face-lift' in that it closes and tightens your pores.

You will need:
Two egg whites
Two teaspoons of ground almonds

Whip the egg whites until they are thick, fold in the almonds and apply.

Leave for 15 minutes and gently wash off.

Honey and avocado face-pack
Avocados are your skin's best friend because they are so rich in vitamin E. They make wonderfully soothing face-packs for stressed and weary skin and are ideal for relieving that wind-burnt winter feeling.

You will need:
One ripe avocado (ideally organic)
One generous teaspoon of honey
One teaspoon of lemon juice

Mash the avocado and gently stir in the honey and lemon juice.

Apply and leave for ten minutes.

Massage

Massage is a particularly wonderful way to while away a couple of hours, particularly if your whole weekend is dedicated to making your body feel better.

Book a massage at a clinic you can easily reach because a three-hour round trip in a succession of buses and trains is hardly conducive to making you feel relaxed. Even better, arrange for someone to visit you at home. Masseurs can be found in the Yellow Pages or via local clinics.

NB: Don't invite a complete stranger to your home. Find a masseur through a friend or a trusted organization.

If you are a little bamboozled by the kinds of massage on offer these days, here is a brief run-down of what is available to help you choose what would be of most benefit.

Aromatherapy

This is a very gentle form of massage and utilizes essential oils extracted from aromatic plants and herbs. It is based on the belief that smells are very important to your well-being, inducing moods of calm and helping us to re-orientate ourselves.

If that sounds a little unlikely then consider how strongly you react to repulsive smells – they can even make you sick! Smells we like can have an equally powerful effect for the good.

Your aromatherapist will ask you about your health

in order to deduce what oils would suit you best. For instance, some oils are not advisable for pregnant women while some are very good for combating the ill-effects of pollution and smoking.

Once an oil (or, more usually, a blend of oils) has been selected, it is mixed into a carrier oil such as almond or wheatgerm oil, and applied to the skin. Essential oils should never be applied to the skin undiluted.

The massage itself, which may concentrate on the legs or wherever you need attention, is very soothing and light.

Chiropractic

Daniel Palmer, a 19th-century healer, developed Chiropractic when he deduced that any imbalance or displacement in the skeleton prevented the nerves from functioning normally, resulting in pain and/or illness.

A chiropractor helps to relieve pain by manipulation of the body, and is especially effective in combating neck and back problems. Chiropractors are often sought by those suffering severe back problems or whiplash injuries.

An initial consultation will cover your immediate and long-term health issues, and may require an X-ray to check for bone disease of any kind.

Your GP can refer you or recommend you to a good chiropractor – a far safer idea than jotting down the numbers on cards in your local health shop.

Reflexology

Traditional Chinese medicine holds that zones on the soles of our feet relate to internal and external zones in the body. If any of these zones become blocked, illness and a lack of well-being are the result.

To unblock them, the reflexologist attends to the areas of the foot relating to the problem. Thus, manipulating a certain part can help to ease tension headaches while another area corresponds to the intestines, where a little attention can help ease ailments such as constipation.

Odd as it may sound to the uninitiated, it is a delightful experience to have a skilled professional give you a foot rub.

Not only that, many people find it very effective – including an ancient Egyptian doctor from 2330 BC who had paintings depicting a reflexology session in his tomb.

Shiatsu

'Shi' is the Japanese word for finger while 'atsu' means touch but when you put them together you get more than just a massage. This ancient system is designed to steer the body towards healing itself and is particularly effective in dealing with those 'niggling' health problems – such as sleeplessness or back pain – that defy orthodox western treatment.

The massage will help to channel 'chi' – the eastern word for the body's self-generated energy – to where it is most needed. This stimulates the body to tackle the underlying problem, manifested in these symptoms, rather than simply attending to the immediate.

Sunday

On rising
As with Saturday, drink a glass of hot water and lemon juice on rising.

If you feel sleepy, then relax and go back to bed for a while. Don't sleep the whole day of course, but a couple of extra hours won't do you any harm.

If you know you have a busy day ahead tomorrow, make life easier for yourself by laying out the clothes you need for the morning and having everything ready.

You will feel truly refreshed on Monday morning but that's no excuse for leaving everything to the last minute!

The Detox
Weight-Loss Plan

OBESITY is set to become the West's biggest health problem. Not only are increasing numbers of adults entering the seriously overweight zone, but increasing numbers of children are too, which means we are storing up problems for the future.

The fat epidemic

It seems absurd, given that we know the health risks associated with being overweight and that we know what to do to avoid being overweight, but still our combined weight continues its upward trajectory.

Why? It's partly because of easy access to food. If we had to grow, harvest and prepare every ounce of nourishment that passed our lips, it's a guarantee we would eat less.

We would eat more natural foods, prepared with fewer chemical additives and less laden with fat.

Instead, we buy food ready prepared from the supermarket. To keep it fresh tasting, the bread we eat is already salted and sugared and packed with E-numbers, while our fruit and vegetables are irradiated to give them longer life, or peeled and chopped and shoved into tins.

This ensures that we develop an unnatural taste for highly seasoned, 'perfected' food and turn our noses up at dirty organic carrots growing in bizarre shapes and lumpy home-made bread. The reason, for instance, that the peas we buy are always bright green is because market testing showed that consumers simply wouldn't buy the uncoloured variety – in its natural state, a pea is a dull grey-green colour.

We are brought up with the idea that food is easy to get and should always look like it does on the food label. Unfortunately, this means that we eat a diet that is low in nutrition but high in chemicals and added sugars and fats, these latter contributing to our burgeoning weight problem.

But why do we eat so much of this rubbish? Because food manufacturers want us to.

They need to make money so they bombard us with advertizing to induce us to eat not only at mealtimes, but also between meals, while we watch TV, when we see friends and when we want to celebrate our successes or console ourselves after our disasters.

Food is even being advertized as a way of boosting out sex lives. One recent ice-cream campaign featured slinky models seducing each other with spoonfuls of high fat, high sugar dessert. The reality, of course, is that if they really ate as much of this stuff as the commercial suggests, they would long since have lost their status as sex objects! But then, when did advertizing ever touch base with reality?

It is no coincidence that the USA, where food advertizing is almost ubiquitous, has the collective waistline to match.

The other major cause of our weight problem is the sedentary nature of our lifestyles. Forty years ago, we burnt off 25% more calories than we do today. This statistic accounts for a lot of excess weight. These days, we take the car rather than walk a mile into town. We step into the lift rather than waste ten minutes climbing the stairs. We shove all our clothes into the washing machine and press a button rather than hauling it to a laundry to do it by hand.

Of course, no one would wish to return to the

dreary days of cleaning carpets with tea-leaves and a brush and dustpan. But the truth is that we don't make up the difference in other, more enjoyable activities.

In fact, many gyms rely on the fact that at least a third of the people who pay for membership never actually attend. Otherwise the gym would be jam-packed!

Even worse, our children take much less exercise than previous generations, eschewing games of football in the street for long hours playing computer games. The result is fat teenagers who grow into unhealthy, overweight and discontented adults.

The diet epidemic

Bearing this in mind, surely it is a good thing that we have a multi-million pound diet industry to hand?

Well, not really.

Commercial diets are generally based on the principle of quick, impressive weight loss. That is why we want to buy them. Every new diet, whether it is a Hollywood celebrity diet rumoured to have got a five star actress into a size six dress, or a pre-packed milk shake diet guaranteed to be hassle-free and big on taste, is geared to the quick fix mentality.

If we can send a man to the moon and go from 0 to 60 in ten seconds, why can't we cure a little weight problem between now and next week?

The problem is that the weight lost is almost always quickly regained. Research has shown that most successful slimmers regain and even increase on the weight they lose as a result of quick-fix diets. Which is why so many of them become 'yo-yo' dieters, their weight soaring one year and falling away the next.

Not only is this process distressing and boring, it is very bad for your heart, which doesn't appreciate the strain of being fat alternating with the strain of being hungry.

The reason lost weight returns with such a vengeance is that, when you suddenly deprive your body of calories, it thinks it is undergoing famine conditions and works on conserving energy.

It does this by lowering the body's metabolism.

Thus someone who regularly burns off 2,500 calories a day finds themselves burning off only 1,750 after a couple of days of minimal eating. Which means that, when they return to regular eating, they do not burn off their habitual intake and instead begin storing the excess as fat.

Exercising in a bid to boost this lowering metabolism helps to an extent but too much exercise on an empty stomach results in your body burning off its muscle reserve rather than its fat. This may sound frustrating and perverse but it makes sense biologically. Your body wants to stay alive and warm, and holding onto its fat is one way of ensuring survival.

Unfortunately, we don't seem to learn and the vastly expanding slimming business is cashing in on our vastly expanding, collective waistline.

A long-term weight loss plan

A word to the wise – don't call it a diet.

The best, possibly the only, way to lose weight successfully is to do it slowly and as part of a healthy, long-term eating plan. Don't call it a diet because, if you want to stay slim for the rest of your life, you are going to have to adhere to its principles for the rest of your life.

Don't despair. This is not nearly as draconian as it sounds. You won't be hungry for the rest of your life, or forced to eat celery and cottage cheese. In fact, you need not be hungry or doomed to dull foods at all.

But you will have to say goodbye to a lot of bad habits.

That said, a habit is just something you do a lot and if you start making healthy choices on a regular basis, this will become a replacement habit.

In fact, as you lose weight and start to feel the added benefits of increased energy, a better complexion, better health and more confidence, any passion for cheeseburger and chips while slumped in front of the television will quickly fade.

As they say – nothing tastes as good as the feeling of being slim.

The kick start

It's a funny thing but most of us, when we've vowed to go on a diet, prepare for it by stuffing ourselves full of the foods we don't think we will be able to eat again!

Psychologically this is great, because we are so engorged with food we crave a day of water and fresh air. But in terms of your new regime and its potential success, it stinks. Apart from anything else, a day or two of bingeing means that the first two to three days of your diet are spent recovering from that excess.

So if you are serious about shifting the flab, get a grip. By all means go for a nice meal or enjoy a last bar of chocolate but don't sabotage your first week by going crazy with the deep-fried peanut butter and banana baguettes – a thousand-calorie favourite of the late, and latterly very fat, Elvis Presley.

A great way to get going is to begin with a juice fast. For this you will of course need a juicer, plenty of fresh fruit and vegetables and, ideally, a couple of relaxing days on hand.

This is not recommended if you have any health problems, particularly those relating to the heart. If you are concerned, check with your GP first.

Furthermore, if you begin the fast and find that you feel dizzy or weak, return to solid foods immediately. This is designed to give you a kick start, not a kicking!

The juice fast

Freshly squeezed juice is an ideal food because it means you consume lots of fruit and vegetables in their raw state. You have no doubt heard plenty of testimonies to the near magical properties of raw food but, in simple terms, it is good because it is at its most nutritionally rich.

As soon as you start to cook food, it loses a little of this goodness – though some forms of preparation are more ravaging than others.

However, cooking didn't come about by accident. It exists to make food more palatable and enjoyable and it is therefore extremely unlikely that you will develop a taste for raw food full-time. Therefore don't worry if the thought of carrot and celery juice never gets you quite as excited as a bacon sandwich with mustard.

Juice is also good because it is a very pure food. It tastes great without any added salt or sugar and therefore a couple of days on it will help to clear your palate and open the way for a less seasoned and toxifying diet in the future.

In fact, if you never ate sugar again, you would not be depriving your body of any nutrition at all. Refined white sugar only entered the human diet relatively recently – which is quite surprising when you consider that it is contained in so many foods, from baked beans to pan bread – and provides nothing but empty calories and a host of health problems.

Excessive sugar in the diet can lead to dental problems, diabetes, heart problems and hypoglycemia, also known as low blood sugar. Learn instead to use small doses of honey, a natural sugar and a sweeter one, spoonful for spoonful. Fruits also contain a natural sugar, so utilize them when you want a dose of sweetness. Currants, for instance, are ideal sweeteners in puddings and are good for reducing the bitterness of stewed apples.

If you habitually shake a little salt over your food, consider giving the salt cellar the elbow along with the sugar bowl.

We do need some salt in our diet, particularly when we sweat, but too much salt in the diet has been linked with high blood pressure, insomnia, kidney problems and heart disease.

In fact, most foods contain salt already, as you will discover. A salt-free day is all it takes to realize that foods really do have a taste of their own. If you must have salt on occasion, consider switching to a low sodium salt or a herb salt.

Coffee and tea are absolutely out during the juice fast, as are alcohol and smoking.

Great juice ingredients

Alfalfa: although a little too much like rabbit food for some people's tastes, alfalfa is a real tonic if you're feeling bilious.

Apples: wonderfully cleansing thanks to the

detoxifying properties of the pectin they contain. They are also easily digestible, very thirst quenching and help to reduce stomach acidity. They are in season in the autumn and choosing organic is particularly recommended. Make an ideal basis for many juice combinations and, when sweetened with a little honey, makes a delicious juice all on its own.

Beetroot: this distinctly old-fashioned vegetable has been used in cookery for over two millennia. Though its taste is a little powerful for some palates, it is great with carrots and cabbage in a juice, is rich in B vitamins and has strong antioxidant properties.

Cabbage: try to dispel all school dinner associations, as cabbage is one of those wonder vegetables that persuades toxins to stick to it as it passes through the body. It is also believed to be very effective at combating digestive problems and treating acid stomachs. As it is filling but low in calories, it is a must for a weight loss detoxer.

Carrot: found it in almost every juice recipe and no wonder. It tastes great and is packed with vitamin C and beta-carotene. It is often used in anti-cancer diets thanks to its rich stock of vitamin E, which some believe is resistant to cancer cells. It also helps to relieve constipation, making it a detox must.

Coriander: ideally, buy a coriander plant and chop off leaves as and when you need them. A small handful of leaves gives a lift to all kinds of dishes, particularly curries, while a couple of leaves turns a regular juice into an exotic drink. Renowned for its digestive properties, coriander is also rich in vitamin A.

Cucumber: makes a very refreshing juice, particularly when blended with lettuce, parsley and tomatoes. It is rich in B vitamins and exceptionally low in calories, so a good one for dieters.

Fenugreek: much used in Indian cookery, fenugreek is iron-rich and helps to stimulate the production of bile, making it a good aid to digestion. Nice taste too.

Fig: fresh ripe figs are hard to come by but if you see them, buy them. They make a rich juice, which offers a natural relief to constipation and keeps the liver refreshed. If you cannot find fresh, then dried figs soaked overnight can be blended, along with the water they soaked in, to make a great juice.

Garlic: the scourge of vampires is renowned for its health-giving properties. It is great for the purposes of detoxifying in that it helps to relieve water retention and stimulates the liver. It is also very good for the blood, helping to combat high blood pressure and thickening artery walls. Recommended for daily use.

Ginger: a little grated ginger adds warmth and spice to any juice but its benefits extend beyond taste alone. It is a great aid to digestion (which is why drinking ginger tea is so beneficial after a big meal) and helps to alleviate wind.

Grapes: a great source of potassium, while black grapes in particular are a powerful source of antioxidants. One word of warning though – grapes are particularly susceptible to airborne pollutants and pesticide residues so you must always wash them well before eating, even organic ones.

Guava: not easy to find, but worth it. They are rich in vitamin C, a vitamin the body cannot store, so make sure you get your Recommended Daily Allowance (RDA). Don't allow it to become too ripe as this reduces the levels of vitamin C.

Lemon: detoxers should always have lemons in the house as they make great fat-free salad dressing, can be squeezed over grilled fish and used to pep up drinks. It is recommended for cold-sufferers and appears to be useful in combating rheumatism as it stimulates the liver to expel toxins – which is why it is such a good detox staple too.

Melon: the taste of summer, it goes well with all summer fruits. It is a good antioxidant as well as being a rich source of vitamin C. Some research suggests it might also be good for relieving the symptoms of eczema.

Mint: as with coriander, this should be one of your window sill herbs. As well as giving a kick to all kinds of juices, mint helps to alleviate indigestion by stimulating the digestive tract.

Onions: if you're always catching colds, it's time you got to know your onions. They form the basis of many dishes because of their versatility and taste but they also have medicinal properties in abundance. They are a good decongestant, have bags of vitamin C, help to lower cholesterol and prevent the blood from becoming too 'sticky' and viscous.

Orange: like apples, they contain pectin, making them a useful aid when combating constipation. High levels of pectin are also believed to lower the body's cholesterol level. They are also good antioxidants. Dyspepsia, caused by undigested food lingering too long in the digestive tract and causing wind, is also said to be relieved with a regular dose of oranges.

Pears: if you crave the kind of instant energy that sugar gives you, have a pear. Most of its calories are in the form of natural sugars so it works as a pick-me-up. It is one of the least allergenic of foods too, so it's useful for those who are troubled by food intolerances.

Papaya: this sweet juicy fruit hails originally from Mexico and is fast becoming fashionable over here. Like many orange-coloured fruits, it is a rich source of beta-carotene, which means it is a good antioxidant. It contains the enzyme papain, similar to pepsin, which is produced by the human digestive system to break down proteins, and means it may go some way to assisting the body in its digestion. Some research suggests that papaya also has pain-relieving properties, making it a good choice for days when you are feeling below par. Some claims have been made for its anti-ageing properties too.

Pineapple: for years it was hard to find anything other than the tinned and chunked variety but fresh pineapples are increasingly easy to find in greengrocers and supermarkets. When they are ripe you should be able to pull out a leaf from the top with relative ease. Though they require a good deal of chopping and washing, they are worth it because of the enzyme bromelain, which breaks down proteins. This aids the body's own digestion of proteins but, though some diet gurus may claim otherwise, it does not contain any magical weight loss properties.

Pomegranate: this delightful little fruit is said to boost brain power. That aside, it is a good antioxidant and helps to relieve biliousness and other ailments associated with poor digestion. However, it does have quite a subtle taste so be careful not to overwhelm it in juice with stronger tastes.

Pumpkin: whatever you do, avoid the giant, round pumpkins you get in supermarkets around 31st October. These 'forced' fruits are grown purely for the ease with which they can be carved into Halloween lanterns and the fruit inside is generally tasteless and foamy – enough to put you off pumpkins for life. But organic pumpkins are delicious and sweet, and contain lots of vitamin A and beta-carotene. The seeds are wonderful too. Dry and roast them and eat them cold with cereal or natural yoghurt.

Squashes such as acorn and butternut squash are also pumpkins strictly speaking and have the same properties.

Radishes: members of the cruciferous family, which includes broccoli, cauliflower and brussels sprouts. Regarded largely as a salad vegetable, radishes are used in herbal medicine as a diuretic, making them useful for those suffering from water retention.

Raspberries: as well as being a real treat, raspberries have long since been used by naturopathic healers to treat digestive and liver disorders. They really do help to cleanse the system. They also contain lots of vitamin C and can help to soothe cystitis and relieve diarrhoea.

Spinach: though it isn't as rich in iron as Popeye's endorsement might suggest, spinach is good as a source of carotene and vitamin C and helps to stimulate peristalsis, thus relieving constipation.

Strawberries: have a higher concentration of vitamin C than any other fruit and, like raspberries, have long been used by naturopathic healers for cleansing the system. Beware however – some people find they are extremely allergic to strawberries so, no matter how tempted, don't overdo it.

Tomatoes: contain carotenoids, which act as powerful antioxidants and therefore help to alleviate toxin overload. Antioxidants are also believed to help prevent cancer. They are very low in calories but high in vitamins C and E. For a sweet flavour, choose yellow tomatoes or cherry tomatoes. However, mouth ulcers and eczema could be the result of a tomato allergy so go easy to begin with.

Turmeric: this is a popular ingredient in Indian cookery and is valued for its rich yellow colour. Add a pinch or two to vegetable juices as it is renowned for its liver-cleansing properties. Too much can leave a bitter taste, so use sparingly.

A typical day's juice-fasting

On waking
Drink a glass of hot water with some freshly squeezed lemon juice. Do a series of stretches as outlined in the seven-day detox plan.

Breakfast
Juice made from one carrot, one apple and an orange.

Mid-morning
Take a brisk ten-minute walk. Don't attempt to do any vigorous exercise as your body has enough to

cope with. Instead, take it easy, enjoy being in the fresh air and take deep breaths as you go.

As soon as you get home, pour yourself a long glass of cold water and slowly sip it until it's gone. You MUST drink eight glasses a day so always have water to hand and get into the habit of sipping.

Lunch
Juice made with a handful of fresh spinach, which is rich in iron and a great detoxifier, a clove of crushed garlic, a squeeze of lemon, 100g of cooked beetroot (not pickled), two sticks of celery and three carrots.

Mid-afternoon
Enjoy a cup of dandelion coffee and, if you feel hungry, have an apple or a pear. Or stick both in the juicer along with a squeeze of lemon juice.

Use your time to give your skin a good body brush before having a relaxing soak in the tub. Don't have the water above body temperature or you will emerge feeling washed out and exhausted.

Afterwards, apply body lotion to your skin, massaging it in properly so that your circulation benefits too. Then drink another long glass of water and relax over a magazine or an afternoon film.

Dinner
Eat early because you want to fit in another juice fix before bed! This time, try a combination of half a

small red cabbage, two or three apples and half a bulb of fennel. It is surprisingly tasty and very good for you.

Supper
Aim to drink this about an hour and a half before bed. A juice of strawberries and peaches is very refreshing and light.

Bed
Retire early and get a good night's sleep. You'll need it!

The next step
Whatever you do, don't stay on juices for more than two days. Your body is designed to eat solid food so don't deny it.

The seven-day detox is the next step for you, followed by the longer term guidelines. But remember, this is not a crash diet and there is no merit in going hungry for long periods of time. Starving yourself will only make you discouraged and lethargic.

Once you have completed the first seven days, you must start taking exercise regularly. The fitness plan outlined later in the book is perfect for absolute beginners and will not only help you tone up as you lose weight, it will increase the speed at which you lose fat.

Weight loss should occur no more rapidly than

one to two pounds a week. If you have a great deal of weight to lose, you may lose four to fourteen pounds very rapidly and then the rate at which you lose weight will slow down significantly.

However, if you feel at all unwell or lightheaded, it is vital that you consult your GP and discuss your symptoms with him or her. The chances are they will be delighted that you have decided to take your health seriously and will offer good advice and encouragement, so don't feel hesitant about seeking advice.

Learn to listen to your body

The reason a person becomes overweight is because they eat more calories than they burn off. That's all. Some of us are genetically more inclined to be fat than others but that's because we're genetically inclined to burn less calories.

The secret to maintaining your ideal weight is in listening to your body and understanding when it needs fuel and when that urge to eat a hotdog in the middle of the afternoon is just a response to stress.

But tuning into your physical needs can be a difficult business and will take concentration and time. Our eating habits have become distorted thanks to the pressure of advertizing, cultural rituals such as Christmas and birthdays and, perversely enough, the idealization of thinness which prompts us to begin dieting and thus muck around with our perception of food.

But don't be discouraged – a natural relationship with food can be recovered.

Start by paying attention at mealtimes. Eat slowly, savour what you're eating and be aware of when you are full. Not groaningly full, but just at that point where you would be more comfortable stopping than continuing to eat. And stop.

Fast eaters lose out here because there is a little delay between swallowing your food and a sense of fullness being conveyed to your brain. If you eat slowly, there is time for that message to get to there. If you wolf, you will have reached fullness long before you realize it and, consequently, you will continue to overeat.

Learn to distinguish between real hunger and other physiological triggers. For instance, maybe you're just tired? We often eat in response to weariness, to keep us going while we finish typing up that report or sit out the last hours of a shift. If you really can't take a rest instead, have a piece of fruit or a walk in the fresh air – both activities will revive you.

Thirst is another symptom commonly mistaken for hunger. Have a glass of water if you are at all unsure – your 'hunger pangs' may disappear instantly!

Psychological triggers can also make us eat.

For instance, when we feel bad about ourselves, we often turn to food because it is a guaranteed way to improve our mood – if only while we are actually in the process of eating. Afterwards is a different matter: it can often make us feel worse.

If you think low self-esteem might be prompting you to eat when you are not genuinely hungry, it is time you did something positive or you will never break out this vicious circle.

Exercise, boringly enough, will improve your self-esteem enormously. Not just because it releases endorphins in your brain that make you feel good, but also because it increases your energy levels and improves your skin tone and waistline. If you're a real couch potato, then building up a regular exercise routine and sticking to it will give you an enormous sense of achievement too.

Learn to be good to yourself in ways that don't involve eating. Book yourself into the hairdressers or buy yourself something new to wear, or a glossy magazine. Take a day off work and spend it wandering round an art gallery or window shopping or sitting in the garden with a good book.

Susie Orbach, author of *Fat Is A Feminist Issue*, advises women who are stuck in the dieting/binging cycle, to stop thinking of themselves as imperfect and to make the most of who they are *right now*. Instead of thinking, 'There's no point in wasting money buying clothes when I'm fat', think 'I'm going to buy myself something so I look the very best I can.'

Dressing for today, making the most of yourself as

you are, really can help you lose weight, because it raises your sense of self, and therefore makes you more inclined to take care of yourself and want to be the best you can be.

Each and every one of us has a 'set point' — an ideal weight at which our body functions at its best. You will only ever find out what it is if you learn to eat when you are hungry, and to eat the foods that your body actually wants.

And you might find that you simply were not intended to be as skinny as a rake. But what you will find is that it feels great to be functioning on all cylinders.

The detox plan assists this process by weaning you off unnatural foods, such as sweets and salt-laden takeaways. Eating real food is an essential step in learning to distinguish real hunger and reaching your real weight.

Your very good health

The beauty of this form of losing weight is that not only is it viable as a long-term eating plan, but that it is so wonderfully beneficial in so many other ways too.

Because fresh food is so rich in vitamins and because your liver will be fed all the right things, your health will improve enormously. After the initial few weeks, you will probably find that you are much less prone to catching colds, that you sleep better and that your levels of anxiety have dropped significantly.

The Ultimate Hangover Cure

NOT feeling so good this morning? There are few of us who can honestly claim to have never suffered a hangover. Though some of us visit that particular region of ill health a little more often than others.

The symptoms include:

Headache
Caused by the diuretic effect of alcohol, which leads

to dehydration, and the presence of congeners, the substances in alcoholic drinks that give them their colour and taste.

Nausea
Caused by the stomach lining being irritated by too much alcohol.

Weariness
Caused by the liver being oversubscribed with alcohol to process and thus unable to convert food into glycogen for energy.

Never again!
Then there is the confusion, the pasty complexion, the raging desire to eat everything you can get your hands on and the conviction that you will never, ever drink again.

But it will do your health the world of good if you give it up for a few weeks, even a couple of months. Because, despite the claim that a glass of red wine is good for your heart, the truth is that alcohol does you no real good at all. It has no nutritional content, it doesn't protect your heart, and even its ability to relax you is counterbalanced by its ability to plunge you into a deep depression.

It causes irritability, nervous tension and insomnia because, like caffeine, it stimulates the secretion of adrenaline. Which is why, the night after the night before, it can be difficult to sleep; your brain is still 'buzzing' with artificial stimulant even though your body, thanks to the pounding your liver is taking, is worn out.

Alcohol taken in excess can also cause the accumulation of fatty deposits around the heart and liver and lead to an impairment of the immune function.

Alcohol is bad news and you can live without it.

So, if you are reading this with a hangover gently pounding through your head, here's what to do first:

Drink water, and lots of it

Have a glass of the stuff beside you all day and don't stop just because you're passing urine regularly and it looks clear. Your body is simply processing it in order to flush out some of the rubbish you've been drinking.

Eat

Your body craves calories when you're hangover because its vitamin and mineral cupboard has been stripped bare by last night's drinking binge. Drinking alcohol depletes the body's stock of vitamins A, B and C, magnesium, zinc and essential fatty acids.

And a fry-up is not going to help, no matter how tempting it looks.

Instead, make yourself some porridge. It's easy to digest and is rich in the body's favourite fuel –

carbohydrates. Instead of adding sugar or salt, mash in a banana while it's still hot. This will give you a little energy and feed your body some essential vitamins.

Later on, make yourself some vegetable soup for a fix of vitamin C.

Sleep
If at all possible, rest up for the day. Your body is exhausted.

Take a milk thistle supplement to help your liver do its work.

Drink juice
Not just because it adds variety but also because it will boost your vitamin C stocks. Leslie Kenton recommends apple juice, diluted with a little water, because of the detoxification properties of pectin. Pear juice is just as good.

Get a little exercise
Nothing too strenuous, just a 20-minute walk.

Boost your blood sugar
But not with a king-size chocolate bar. Instead, have a glass of hot water with lemon juice and a spoonful of honey. Not exciting, but it will make you feel better.

Watch a feel-good movie
Hangovers can be very depressing affairs so don't

make it worse by berating yourself. Watch *It's A Wonderful Life* and promise to take better care of yourself in future.

Have a bath
The steam will encourage your body to detox that little bit quicker. Add a couple of drops of lavender and bergamot essential oils to the water as this will also speed up the detox process and help you sleep later on.

The first week
If your alcohol intake has been particularly heavy lately, the first few 'dry' days can be rather wearisome. But if you follow the seven-day detox, the side effects will diminish much more rapidly than if you were to stick to comfort foods and industrial quantities of tea and coffee.

Appearance-wise, you might notice that your eyes are rather puffy. This is a sign that there are a lot of toxins in your body and can be unsightly.

A cooling gel eye mask, available from chemists, will help reduce the swelling and also doubles up as an effective headache soother. Cold used teabags are also good.

Your skin may look rather grey and even break out in spots. Again, it's just a symptom of a toxic build up so ride with it. Face-packs are great for putting a little colour back into washed-out complexions as they boost the circulation but be warned, they will also bring spots to the surface.

You may experience prolonged bouts of indigestion. If so, avoid eating difficult to digest foods such as pulses and beans. But do eat plenty of fruit and vegetables as this will ensure your bowel movements are regular which, in turn, will help to alleviate your indigestion.

Foods such as cabbage and brown rice will aid this process as they draw toxins from the gut during the process of digestion.

After two to three days, you will feel remarkably better but don't slip back to your usual routine. The longer you stay with the detox programme, the greater chance you are giving your liver to make a full recovery.

It will also help you break that it's-Friday-so-I-must-have-a-gin-and-tonic habit. Find alternatives for a few weeks, such as an evening class or the cinema or catching up on programmes you missed through the week with a Friday night video binge. It is truly amazing how interesting life can be beyond the four walls of the wine bar.

A new way of drinking

You could live without it forever but, chances are, you will make a return to drinking. So make plans to do it sensibly.

Detox

Unlike the French, we Brits have a rather unhealthy relationship with booze. Where they regard it as something to be enjoyed regularly but in extreme moderation, we tend to veer between total abstemiousness and happy hour bonanzas.

So think like a French person. Have a glass of red with the evening meal and then cork the bottle. You can have another one tomorrow.

When you go to a party, have a couple of drinks and then switch to soft drinks or glasses of water.

Never drink on an empty stomach or when you are tired.

Don't plan whole evenings in the pub. Go for an hour and then go to the pictures.

Learn to savour the taste of a good wine or a nicely mixed vodka and tonic or a half pint of real ale.

And keep to the recommended units per week – 14 for women, 21 for men.

Remember, drinking can be a very pleasant activity, particularly when done in the company of good friends. Don't spoil it by letting minor bad habits grow into major problems.

Detox Your Environment

WE LIVE very fast, busy lives in the twenty-first century. The roads are full of angry car drivers hurrying to the next traffic jam, the skies are filled with planes criss-crossing the globe at ever increasing speeds, we all have televisions and microwave ovens and mobile phones and e-mail addresses. We buy instant food and expect things to happen *now*. We don't have time to wait.

But all this hurry comes at a price.

Not only are we stressing ourselves out trying to fit too much activity and achievement into too little time, the environment is bearing the brunt of it too. Too many cars on the roads equals too many fumes in the air we breathe. Planes are even worse.

Computerization, while it makes office life more efficient, exposes us to hazardous toxins; prolonged use of computers has been linked to poor eyesight.

Mobile phones have been controversially linked to cancers and diseases in children – witness the outcry whenever a new mobile phone mast is erected for an idea of how concerned people are becoming.

The mass-market food industry, as well as increasing the use of damaging pesticides, which inevitably enter the food chain, also adds to the world's collective fuel emissions. After all, exotic fruits don't get here by carrier pigeon.

In short, the air we breathe is far from the blissfully pure stuff we'd like it to be. But aside from lobbying the government to reduce fuel emissions in industry and support a proper public transport infrastructure (and these activities are extremely important if we are ever to see change) – what can we do to lessen the impact of it all on our health?

Clearing the air

One strongly recommended way to improve your environment is to invest in an ionizer. These little machines, available from large chemists, remove the charge from ions.

This may sound like double Dutch, unless you know that in busy environments where there is a lot of machinery and traffic, there is a preponderance of positively charged ions. Too many of these make us listless and overwrought.

Negative ions, which are found in abundance at the seaside because the sea removes the charge from ions, are invigorating. An ionizer will increase the amount of negative ions in your immediate atmosphere, leaving you feeling a great deal more alert.

Plants are also very helpful, particularly if you work at a computer. They feed off carbon dioxide and expel fresh oxygen into the air. They are also rather good at absorbing toxins from the atmosphere – spider plants especially.

However, these are only tiny measures compared to actually getting some fresh air. Even in a city it is better to be outdoors than in. Homes are full of potentially toxic substances, from furniture polish to bathroom cleaner, and offices even more so. While you are indoors, keep a window open, but try to escape every three hours or so for 15 minutes of air.

However, if you go running, health experts warn against running beside busy roads or – perhaps surprisingly – through urban woodland as pollutants gather in areas that are sheltered.

Ideally, try to increase your visits to the open countryside and the seaside. And do the rest of the planet a favour – don't take the car, take the bus.

The toxic home

As mentioned above, the home is one of the most toxic places you could live in, but there is an abundance of improvements you can make, opening windows being the first and easiest. Even in winter, ensure you air every room you plan to spend any time in for at least half an hour a day. Not only does this allow fresh air to circulate, it is very refreshing, as we tend to cocoon ourselves in cold weather without realizing that in so doing we are breathing in stale air.

Be rigorous about having your gas pipes checked for leaks and your plumbing checked for lead. Even a small amount of either substance can be fatal.

When it comes to cleaning products, it makes sense to take the green option. Low impact products don't just reduce the level of harmful by-products being washed back into the water supply or expelled into the air, they are better for you too. Your local health shop will stock everything you need, from phosphate-free washing powder to chemical-free cleansers.

Unsurprisingly, paint is a particularly unpleasant substance to have around but petrochemical-free paints are readily available now. So next time you decorate, consider whether you want to be breathing in petrochemical by-products for the next few months, or whether you want a truly fresh, clean start.

Give up smoking

The best way of improving your environment is to give up smoking. It is the single most important thing you can do for your health, instantly relieving your body of some three thousand-plus toxins at a stroke.

Do we need to add that smoking is linked with a broad range of cancers, that it can cause heart and respiratory disease, that it accelerates the ageing process, yellows your teeth, sours your breath, shrinks your lung capacity, ruins your sleep, your concentration and your digestion and costs a fortune into the bargain?

But giving up, of course, is a thousand times more difficult than starting. Which is why such a huge industry has grown up around the quitting issue.

Here is a brief summary of your options:

Acupuncture

This ancient Chinese system involves the insertion of needles into points along the body's 'meridians' through which energy – known as 'chi' – flows. The needles are used to direct energy to where it is needed most at any given time.

Pain signals, sent along nerves to the brain, can be blocked with the use of acupuncture, making it an effective treatment for conditions like rheumatism.

For those seeking to give up smoking, it can alleviate withdrawal symptoms, allowing you to get through those first miserable weeks relatively painlessly.

Aversion therapy

A psychiatric term used to describe the discouragement of an undesirable habit by means of associating it with something deeply unpleasant, like a disgusting smell or nausea. Some people attempt to administer their own by, for instance, smoking twice their daily ration of cigarettes in one sitting to sicken themselves. However, this form of self-administered 'therapy' is rarely effective.

Hypnotherapy

The American Journal of Psychology noted that hypnotherapy appears to be the most successful means to giving up the weed, and anecdotal evidence is impressive.

A typical session will begin with the hypnotherapist asking you to detail your smoking habits, what prompted you to start and what has now prompted you to want to stop. His/her intention is to provide you with a hypnotherapy session geared specifically to your needs.

They will then ask you to relax, possibly counting you down to a state of deep relaxation.

Once you are ready, the therapist will talk to you about smoking and about your reasons for wanting to quit and this will help to plant the seed of determination in your mind. After all, giving up is easy when you're determined. It's when your determination wavers in the face of temptation that it gets tough. Hypnotherapy helps you keep your edge.

Nicotine substitutes

Patches and gum can be effective if it is the nicotine you are addicted to, as it administers an increasingly reduced dosage, thus alleviating withdrawal symptoms.

However, such substitutes do not address the psychological side of smoking, the urge to perform your smoking rituals, the social prop many of us find in having a cigarette to hold.

Plus, there's nothing to stop you becoming addicted to patches and gum as well!

Willpower

The most basic of them all and certainly a contributory factor in all successful bids to quit smoking.

Whatever method you choose, help yourself by setting a date for stopping – be it January 1st, your birthday or the day your child starts school. Mark it in your diary and stick to it.

Plan to dismantle your 'psychological cues' – that is, the daily events that mark themselves out as 'cigarette moments'. For instance, if you always light up when you have your morning coffee, ditch the coffee and go for a walk instead. If you always smoke after lunch, go for a swim in your lunch hour or do some (enjoyable) shopping.

Avoid situations where you'll be tempted, at least for the first two to three weeks. And don't go near a pub if you associate that first drink with that first glorious puff.

Be prepared for irritability and indigestion, the two most common side effects of stopping smoking. You may find your sleeping patterns go to the wall too but be assured, once the withdrawal effects have gone, you will sleep better and more regularly than ever.

Guard against weight gain. No matter what you read or hear, be assured that your metabolism does *not* change when you give up smoking. It might be a tiny bit slower, but you can make up the difference with a little exercise.

What *will* change is your appetite, as you will suddenly rediscover what food actually tastes like. You may also find that you want to keep snacking as a substitute for smoking.

Help yourself by stocking up on foods like celery

and carrots, which can be chopped up into crudités and snacked on all day long without doing any damage to your waistline. It may sound dull but, when your newly enhanced taste buds get a load of them, they'll be delighted.

Finally, give yourself a boost by putting aside the money you save on cigarettes and spending it on something wonderfully self-indulgent.

How detox can help

Going on a new diet *and* giving up smoking may sound like madness of the first order but, in fact, it makes a lot of sense.

For one thing, it will associate healthy eating with not smoking.

For another, detox foods, being so rich in vitamins and minerals, will help you replace your body's depleted stocks.

Evidence suggests that smokers are always short of vitamin C: some results suggest smokers have up to 30% less than non-smokers. Eating plenty of fresh fruit and vegetables will get you back to full health.

Ex-smokers will feel the benefit of the detox diet's antioxidants too as, for once, they won't be squandered counteracting the poisons present in cigarette smoke. Citrus fruits, peppers and grapes are particularly recommended for the recently quit smoker.

Wholegrains and lean meat and fish, staples of the detox, help to replace stocks of vitamin B12, which may have been depleted helping the liver to process the cyanide found in cigarette smoke.

Omega-3 oils, found in fish and shellfish, will also restore you.

Thirdly, the detox diet will speed the elimination of harmful toxins from your body, allowing you to enjoy the benefits of giving up smoking all the sooner.

Tips for giving up smoking

Follow the seven-day detox plan, making sure you drink enough water. This will speed up the expulsion of cigarette-related toxins from your body.

Get plenty of fresh air. Take a walk or go for a cycle run every single day.

Take deep breaths. One of the reasons smoking is so relaxing is that, when we inhale, we take a deep inward breath. So learn to do this without the cigarette. Try lighting a candle and sitting down in front of it in a darkened, quiet room. Watch the flame until your mind stops ticking over with thoughts, and begin to take slow deep breaths down into your diaphragm, holding for three to five seconds, and exhaling equally slowly. Do ten to begin with.

Find stress solutions. You smoked when you were stressed, so what are you going to do now? Exercise is the best stress-buster of them all, because it releases endorphins, the body's natural pain-killing chemicals. 20 minutes of vigorous aerobic exercise will calm you down more effectively than 20 cigarettes.

Or you could think back to activities that relaxed you as a child – that is, before you ever smoked. If you used to like drawing or painting, buy yourself some kit and give it a whirl. Or get some good books out the library. Or take up line dancing.

Look after your skin. The skin is the biggest organ in the body and it reflects our state of health like a mirror. Which is why, when you smoke, it goes grey and prematurely lined.

When you stop, help it to recover its vigour. Daily dry skin brushing, regular use of body lotion, massage, toning exercises – they all help pep up the circulation and improve the skin's condition.

The better you look, the less you'll be tempted to undo all your good work and light up.

Recipes

WHAT many people find when they alter their diet is just how few recipes they use on a regular basis. The following recipes are all extremely simple and chosen to give your taste buds as wide a variety as possible.

However, you may have a couple of old stand-bys of your own that you would like to tailor to meet your detox needs. In terms of substitutions, lemon juice generally makes a good stand-in for vinegar, and beetroot for red wine. Barley flour is a good alternative to wheat flour and rice milk can usually be used instead of cow's milk. If not, there is goat's and sheep's milk, which are much easier to digest.

Breads

Yeast-free bread

You will need:
675g wholemeal flour
One and a half teaspoonfuls low sodium salt
450ml water

Combine the flour and salt in a mixing bowl and stir in enough warm water to make a soft dough.

Lift onto a lightly floured surface and knead for five minutes or so and then return to the bowl.

Cover with a damp cloth and leave in a warm place overnight.

Next morning, turn out onto a lightly floured surface again and knead for another five minutes.

Place in a greased 900g loaf tin and leave in a warm place for four hours.

Bake in a preheated oven of 200°C (gas mark 6) for about 30 minutes.

It should then be easily tipped from the tin onto a cooling tray.

Unlike bread made with yeast, it will not rise particularly but it keeps for longer and is surprisingly tasty.

Soda bread

You will need:
450g wholemeal flour
100g fine oatmeal
25g organic butter
One and a half teaspoonfuls of cream of tar-
    tar
One teaspoonful of bicarbonate of soda
A pinch of low sodium salt
450ml water combined with milk

Preheat the oven to 230°C (gas mark 8).

Put the dry ingredients into a mixing bowl and rub in the butter. Then stir in the milk until you get a soft consistency.

Turn the mixture into a lightly greased, medium-sized cake tin and put into the oven for 15 minutes.

Then reduce the heat to 180°C (gas mark 4) for a further 15 minutes and turn out onto a cooling tray.

For best results, eat immediately.

Juices

Apple and Carrot Juice

You will need:
Two apples
One large carrot
50g cooked but not pickled beetroot
50g white grapes
A small chunk of fresh ginger

...and blend!

This is a hugely popular drink and wonderfully rich in vitamin C. Beetroot is also rather helpful if you are suffering from constipation, as it has a gentle laxative effect, or cystitis, as it is believed to relieve some of the symptoms.

Summer Fruit Juice

You will need:
250g strawberries
One nectarine
One eighth slice of honeydew melon
Two or three ice cubes

This is blissful on a summer's day!

Summer Salad Drink

You will need:
Three large tomatoes
Half an English garden lettuce
One third of a cucumber
A small handful of fresh parsley
A small clove of garlic (optional)

This is a great solution to leftover salad syndrome – and very thirst-quenching.

Detox Drink Deluxe

You will need:
Two sticks of celery
Two carrots
One small cooked, but not pickled, beetroot
One orange, peeled and with the pith removed
One apple

This will make two drinks and it is truly scrumptious. It is also superb for giving your detox a boost, and great for hangovers as it puts all the right vitamins back into your system.

Just don't go adding any salt-laden Worcestershire sauce.

Breakfasts

Cornmeal Muffins

You will need:
75g gram or chickpea flour
100g cornmeal
One tablespoonful of wheat-free baking powder
A pinch of low sodium salt
275ml rice milk
One teaspoonful of honey
Two tablespoonfuls of corn oil
One egg

Preheat the oven to 220°C (gas mark 7), and lightly grease a 12-cup muffin tin or line it with 12 paper cases.

Mix the flour, cornmeal, baking powder, honey and salt together in a large bowl. Add the milk, oil and beaten egg and beat together until you've got a smooth batter.

Spoon the mixture into the muffin tin or paper cases and cook in the oven for around 20 minutes until firm to the touch and golden brown.

Delicious when served immediately.

Scrambled Eggs and Ginger

You will need:
Two organic, free range eggs
A dash of soya milk
Olive oil
A small knob of fresh ginger
One clove of garlic, crushed (optional)

Have your ginger and garlic grated and ready – scrambled eggs wait for no one.

Beat the eggs and milk together and pour into a saucepan containing warmed olive oil.

Stirring continuously, add the ginger and garlic.

The mixture will begin to thicken – serve as soon as it is solid enough for your tastes over a couple of rice cakes, adding a little black pepper to season.

Healthy Hash Browns

The ultimate greasy spoon, American-style breakfast can be converted into a healthy option. It's all a question of using your oil sparingly.

You will need:
Two potatoes
One red salad onion
Two free range eggs
Olive oil
Black pepper to taste

Chop up the onion and sauté it in the olive oil until it becomes transparent. Grate the potatoes and add them to the onion, stirring regularly. Sprinkle with a little black pepper and take off the heat.

Now fry the eggs very gently in as little olive oil as you can. Don't let the whites turn brown.

When the eggs are done, serve on top of the hash browns.

Home-Made Muesli

You will need:
250g puffed rice
200g porridge oats
A handful of sunflower seeds
A handful of almonds
A handful of pumpkin seeds
A handful of brazil nuts, roughly chopped up
Two handfuls of currants and raisins
Two apricots or apples, de-seeded and roughly
    diced

This makes a great, crunchy muesli.

Simply mix it all together and serve with a splash of cold soya milk.

Or, to give it a little extra something, soak a portion overnight in some freshly squeezed orange juice, and serve with fresh natural yoghurt.

Soups

Butternut Squash Soup

You will need:
One onion
One butternut squash
Ground cumin
Olive oil
500ml vegetable stock
Sheep's yoghurt, unflavoured

Butternut squash used to be very difficult to find but, thanks to the endorsement of a number of celebrity chefs, you can find them in most supermarkets and greengrocers. They are firm even when ripe.

The cumin really enhances the taste of the squash but be careful not to overdo it as the flavours should be subtle, not overwhelming. Begin by peeling, de-seeding and dicing the squash into one-centimetre cubes.

Put this aside, chop up your onion and sauté in the oil, adding a couple of generous teaspoons of ground cumin. Mix well and allow to cook for a couple of minutes.

Now transfer the mix to your big soup saucepan, pour in the stock and add the squash. Mix and cover, allowing to simmer for 20 minutes or so.

Blend in the liquidizer to get a smooth texture.

Serve with a dollop of fresh yoghurt to give it a creamy taste.

Carrot, Honey and Ginger Soup
Serves 4

You will need:
One onion
Four or five organic carrots, grated
A small piece of fresh ginger
Vegetable stock or salt-free bouillon
Two generous dessertspoonfuls of honey
One dessertspoonful of olive oil

This is so easy to make and is packed with vitamin C.

Chop up the onion and sauté in olive oil until transparent. Add in a pint of stock –

health food shops sell salt-free bouillon, which makes great vegetarian stock in seconds.

Add the carrots.

Allow to cook for 20 minutes then add two generous desert spoonfuls of honey, grate a thumb-sized amount of fresh ginger into the soup and cook for a few minutes more. Liquidize until smooth.

Express Lentil Soup
Serves 2

Lentils are very cleansing and this is a very easy recipe to make.

You will need:
One large onion
One clove of garlic
125g split red lentils
850g vegetable stock
One tablespoonful of lemon juice
Olive oil
Black pepper to taste

Chop the onion and sauté it in the olive oil until it becomes soft, then add in the lentils, stirring for a minute. Now pour in the stock, bring to the boil and leave to simmer for 15 to 20 minutes, or until the lentils are cooked.

You can either liquidize it or serve it as it is with a squeeze of lemon juice and a sprinkling of black pepper. It's that easy.

Parsnip and Apple Soup
Serves 4

You will need:
Four parsnips
Two Bramley cooking apples – don't use ordinary eating apples as much of the apple flavour is lost when cooking.
900ml vegetable stock
Olive oil

A great autumn soup, it tastes sweet and pure.
Begin by chopping up the parsnips and apples.

Lightly sauté them in the olive oil until they begin to soften slightly.

Now pour into a large saucepan, along with the stock and some black pepper to taste.

Allow to simmer gently for about 20 minutes.

Blend in the liquidizer and serve piping hot, garnished with a little chopped fresh parsley.

Salads

There are salads and there are salads. If you're stuck in a cucumber and lettuce rut, read on...

Beetroot, Carrot and Parsnip Salad

This dish is wonderfully colourful and it is crammed with cleansing ingredients.

You will need:
  One raw beetroot, not pickled
  One carrot
  One parsnip
  A small handful of radishes
  A small handful of fresh chives
  Oil and lemon juice dressing (see below)

Grate the beetroot, carrot and parsnip and mix together, gradually adding the dressing. Garnish with the chopped chives and radishes.

Broccoli and Cauliflower Salad

You will need:
One small cauliflower
One large head of broccoli
Oil and lemon juice dressing
Dill weed to season

Steam or par-boil the broccoli and cauliflower. Leave to cool and then cut roughly into largish chunks. Fold in the dressing and a sprinkling of dill weed and serve.

Ginger and Carrot Salad

You will need:
175g carrots
Two medium dessert apples
One teaspoonful of ground ginger or one des-
  sertspoonful of fresh grated ginger
One celery stick
One lemon

Grate the apples and carrots and chop up the celery. Mix the ingredients together, folding in the ginger last. Finish off by squeezing over the juice of the lemon.

Brown Rice Salad

You will need:
100g cooked brown rice
150g garden peas, lightly cooked
Two carrots
One green pepper
The juice of a lemon
Black pepper
Watercress to garnish

De-seed and slice the pepper, then peel and dice the carrots. Mix into the rice, along with the peas and the lemon juice. Garnish with the watercress and serve.

Italian Tomato Salad

You will need:
Four large tomatoes, ideally plum tomatoes
One ripe avocado
One salad onion
A large bunch of fresh basil leaves
Oil and lemon juice dressing
Black pepper to taste

Slice the tomatoes, finely chop the onion, then peel and slice the avocado. Gently combine the ingredients, taking care to keep the tomatoes intact, and serve.

Greek Salad

You will need:
Half a cucumber
Half an iceberg lettuce
One onion
Four large tomatoes
A large handful of black olives, stoned and
   rinsed
100g fresh Feta cheese
One tablespoonful of lemon juice
Two teaspoonfuls of chopped fresh oregano
Olive oil

Cut the cucumber into small chunks, chop up the onion, slice the tomatoes and olives, then cube the cheese.

Place in a bowl and gently fold the ingredients together.

Take the lemon juice, oregano and olive oil and blend together thoroughly.

Shred the washed lettuce, and then place it in a layer along the bottom of the salad bowl. Put the Feta cheese and other prepared ingredients next and drizzle the dressing on top.

Serve immediately or the salad will go soggy.

Spinach and Avocado Salad

You will need:
Two large handfuls of fresh spinach
One large, ripe avocado
A handful of black olives, stoned and rinsed
Two tablespoonfuls of olive oil
One tablespoonful of lemon juice
One clove of garlic, crushed

Chop up the spinach into rough pieces and combine with the sliced avocado and the halved olives.

Mix the olive oil, lemon juice and garlic together and fold into the salad ingredients.

Serve immediately.

Salad Dressing

Oil-free Dressing

You will need:
One tablespoonful of lemon juice
Four tablespoonfuls of unsweetened apple
  juice
A third of a cucumber, with the peel removed
Half a tablespoonful of chopped fresh dill
One garlic clove, crushed
Black pepper to taste

Place all the ingredients in a blender and blend to a smooth paste. Keep refrigerated.

Oil and Lemon Juice Dressing

You will need:
Two tablespoonfuls of olive oil
Juice of one lemon
Black pepper

Mix all ingredients in a container with a lid and shake vigorously before use.

Mayonnaise

You will need:
Two egg yolks
Half a teaspoonful of English mustard powder
A large pinch of low-sodium salt
Two tablespoonfuls of lemon juice
200ml of olive oil

Beat the egg yolks and add in the mustard, salt and lemon juice.

Pour into a blender and, once properly mixed, add the olive oil a little at a time. It is very important that you don't throw in the oil all in one go or the ingredients may separate and you will have to start again.

Keep refrigerated.

Main Meals

Braised Barley with Vegetables
Serves 6

You will need:
Two tablespoonfuls of olive oil
250g pearl barley, available from supermarkets and health shops
250g swede
250g potatoes
One large onion
Two or three carrots
Two or three sticks of celery
Half a pint of vegetable stock
Black pepper to taste

Soak the barley in water overnight. The next day, chop up the onion and sauté in the oil until it turns transparent.

Dice the carrots and cut the celery into centimetre thick slices. Add to the onion and cook for a further few minutes. Dice the swede and potatoes and add these, along with the barley and the water it has soaked in, to the dish and give it a good stir.

Add some black pepper, cover and leave to simmer for 40 minutes, stirring every once in a while.

NB: Instead of salt choose a herb or garlic salt and use it sparingly and in decreasing amounts.

Broccoli with Almonds
Serves 4

You will need:
Two large heads of broccoli
Two garlic cloves, crushed
One tablespoonful of olive oil
One tablespoonful of low salt soy sauce
Two tablespoonfuls of flaked almonds

Wash and de-stem the broccoli and divide the heads into smaller florets.

Add the florets to boiling water and allow to cook for no more than two minutes – you want them to be just tender so that the rich reservoirs of vitamins and minerals are not lost.

Drain the broccoli and place in a wide serving dish.

Heat the olive oil and cook the crushed garlic for two minutes.

Add the almonds and cook for another minute and then pour over the broccoli, using a spoon to ensure the sauce is evenly distributed.

Buckwheat Bake
Serves 4–6

You will need:
Olive oil
One onion
Four large tomatoes
75g buckwheat
30g brown rice
300ml water
A small handful of fresh basil
Black pepper to taste

Preheat the oven to 190°C (gas mark 6).

Chop the onion and tomatoes and then heat a good tablespoonful of oil in a saucepan and add the onion. Sauté for a few minutes, until it becomes transparent, then stir in the buckwheat and rice and cook for a further minute.

Add the water, basil, tomatoes and pepper and bring to the boil. Reducing the heat, cover and allow to simmer until all the liquid has been absorbed. This will take about 20 minutes.

Now turn into a greased, square cake tin of medium size.

Bake in the oven for 30 minutes and serve hot with potatoes or cold with salad.

Cashew Nut Risotto
Serves 2

You will need:
150g brown rice
A handful of unsalted cashews
Two large tomatoes, ideally plum tomatoes
   but must be fresh, not tinned
Half a dozen baby corn
One whole green pepper
One onion
Two dessertspoonfuls of olive oil

This simple dish is surprisingly tasty thanks to the combination of crunchy fresh vegetables and cashews. You can substitute with other vegetables of course – celery works well.

While the rice is cooking, chop up the onion and sauté in the oil until it becomes transparent. Chop up tomatoes roughly, dice the pepper and add to the onion along with the cashews.

Cook gently but don't allow the vegetables to become soft – you want a bit of crunch. Also, the more you cook vegetables, the more nutrients are lost.

Stir into the cooked and drained rice and serve.

Easy Kedgeree
Serves 2

You will need:
200g brown rice
Two fillets of smoked fish
Three hard-boiled, free range eggs
50g frozen garden peas
Two to three boiled potatoes
Olive oil
Fresh parsley

Kedgeree was a popular breakfast dish with the Victorians and no wonder – it will set you up for the toughest of days.

It also doubles as a simple, satisfying dinner. But be sure to use wholegrain rice as, with refined white rice, this basic dish can become seriously bland.

Boil the brown rice and, while it's bubbling away, lightly fry the fish in olive oil until it is opaque. Either that or buy smoked fish that is already cooked.

Your fishmonger will be able to tell you where the fish is smoked and whether the process involves a serious use of chemical dyes or not. Obviously, for the purposes of detox, you want to err on the natural side of things. The good thing about doing this, apart from benefiting your own health, is that it will help to build demand for more natural fish-smoking processes – which is good for everyone.

Shell the eggs and quarter them, and chop up the potatoes into centimetre-sized cubes.

As soon as the rice is cooked, drain it and return to its pot. Flake the fish and gently stir into the rice.

Now add the potatoes and the eggs, taking care not to mash them into the mixture.

Finally, stir in a generous handful of fresh, chopped parsley and serve immediately.

Hummus

You will need:
125 g cooked chick peas
Two tablespoonfuls of tahini – sesame paste,
    available from health food shops
Two tablespoonfuls of lemon juice
Two gloves of organic garlic
Four tablespoonfuls of olive oil

Wash the chick peas and boil in water until tender. Don't throw away the cooking water.

Now add the tahini, lemon juice, garlic and olive oil. Stir roughly and then put into the liquidizer until it becomes a smooth paste.

Use dried rather than tinned chick peas because the tinned varieties tend to have added salt.

This dish is tasty enough without it and is delicious slathered on rice cakes or eaten on its own with a little salad.

Lamb with Rosemary

You will need:
One leg of lamb, boned by the butcher
A large handful of fresh rosemary
One teaspoonful of French mustard
Two teaspoonfuls of olive oil

Preheat the oven to 200°C (gas mark 3).

Use the rosemary as a stuffing for the lamb and coat the outer surface with the French mustard and oil combined.

Put the lamb into the oven in a baking tray and roast for about an hour and a half until well cooked.

Don't allow to burn.

Serve with a salad and boiled new potatoes.

Mushroom and Cashew Nut Stroganoff
Serves 4

You will need:
One onion
350g mushrooms
200g unsalted cashew nuts
One tablespoon of wholewheat flour
150ml water
5ml yeast extract or one teaspoonful of Vegemite

A bay leaf
150ml fresh natural yoghurt
Olive oil

Chop up the onion and sauté in the olive oil until tender. Meanwhile, wash and slice the mushrooms, adding them to the pan when the onion has become transparent. Now add the cashews.

Allow to cook for a couple of minutes before sprinkling over the flour and adding the water, bay leaf and yeast extract. Allow to simmer for two to three minutes and then remove from the heat.

Stir in the yoghurt and serve on a bed of brown rice.

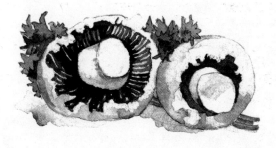

Nut Loaf

You will need:
225g mixed nuts
One onion
One carrot
One stick of celery
One tablespoonful of organic tomato puree
A large can of tomatoes
Two eggs
A large handful of fresh, chopped parsley
Black pepper to taste
Olive oil

Preheat the oven to 220°C (gas mark 7).

Heat the oil in a pan while you chop up the onion, carrot and celery. Add the vegetables and sauté until they are tender.

Add the tomatoes and the tomato puree and cook for a further five minutes.

Beat the eggs and then add in the parsley, pepper and nuts. Add this to the vegetables.

When thoroughly mixed, transfer to a medium-sized, greased loaf tin and cook in the oven for 30 to 35 minutes.

When it's cooked, turn out and allow to cool before adding a few freshly sliced onion rings to garnish.

Serve warm with potatoes or salad, or both.

Orange Chicken

You will need:
Four chicken breasts
One organic orange (in this case it is
    important that the orange is organic
    as you will need the skin, and non-
    organic orange skins often contain
    damaging residues of pesticides)
One garlic clove, crushed
One tablespoonful of fresh basil
Black pepper to taste

Grate the skin of the orange using a reasonably fine grater and then juice the remaining orange. Add together and pile in the garlic, chopped basil and pepper.

Using a sharp knife, make several slits in each chicken breast and then lay them out on a baking tray. Now pour the orange mixture over them, rubbing it into the slits so that the zesty taste of the orange penetrates the flesh. Leave to marinate for ten minutes if possible, then grill the chicken as usual.

Serve immediately, using any mixture left in the tray as a sauce.

Potato Omelette with Herbs
Serves 2–4

You will need:
Four medium-sized potatoes
Three free range organic eggs
Two tablespoons of soya milk
Generous handful of fresh parsley
Two teaspoons of olive oil
Black pepper to taste

Boil and mash the potatoes. As most of the nutritional content of a potato is stored at skin level, try to retain as much of the skin as possible. If you must peel, use a peeler.

Now separate the yolks from the whites of the eggs, beat them and fold into the mashed potato. Add the finely chopped parsley and black pepper.

Whisk the egg whites until they are stiff and add to the mixture.

Heat the olive oil, but not so that it is spitting hot, and pour in the mixture.

Cook for two minutes and then fold over and cook both sides for another minutes or two each.

Salad Nicoise
Serves 2–4

You will need:

A tin of tuna, canned in unsalted water if possible. Otherwise, choose olive or sunflower oil and rinse.

Some small new potatoes

Two free range organic eggs, boiled and shelled

Green beans

One lemon

Half a lettuce or two lettuce hearts

A handful of rocket leaves

A handful of fresh parsley and basil

Olives, green or black depending on preference

Olive oil

Black pepper

This classic salad is wonderfully filling and about as far removed from 'rabbit food' as it's possible to get!

Gently boil the potatoes, having washed them and retained the skins where possible.

While they are cooking, wash and chop up the lettuce and rocket leaves and arrange in your salad bowl. Roughly mix in the herbs and a dessertspoonful of olive oil.

A great chef's tip is to lightly oil the salad bowl with olive oil first so that, when you add in the herbs, they adhere to the sides and are thus distributed throughout the salad rather than in oily 'clots'.

Now drain the tuna, break into chunks and mix into the salad.

Drain the potatoes and allow to cool.

Gently cook the green beans – a few minutes in hot water should do it – and also allow to cool.

Chop the eggs into quarters and add to the salad. Wash the olives and cut in half, and add to the salad.

Chop the potatoes in half, and add to the salad with the green beans, and drizzle everything with freshly squeezed lemon juice.

Add black pepper to taste and serve immediately.

Spicy Lentil Dhal
Serves 6

You will need:
One large onion
Three garlic cloves, crushed
One carrot
250g split red lentils
Two teaspoons of turmeric
Two teaspoons of cumin seeds
Two teaspoons of mustard seeds
One teaspoon of garam masala
Four handfuls of fresh coriander, or two tea-
    spoons of dried coriander (but fresh is best)
One tin of peeled tomatoes, chopped
800ml water
Pinch of chilli powder
A small knob of fresh ginger, grated
One fresh lime or lemon
Olive oil
Black pepper to taste

This dish proves that not all Indian cookery is laden with ghee, the full-fat butter used in many curries and particularly popular amongst us Westerners.

Dhal makes for a very filling evening meal and is particularly tasty served with brown basmati rice.

Using real Indian spices, as opposed to ready mixed curry powder, is a real eye opener to the uninitiated.

You can really taste all the individual flavours. These spices can be found in most supermarkets, Indian grocers and health shops.

Begin by finely chopping the onion and sautéing it in the oil until it is transparent.

Then add the crushed garlic, the cumin and mustard seeds (which will pop, so don't be alarmed), diced carrot and ginger.

Cook for a few minutes, stirring continuously.

Now add the turmeric, which gives the dish its fabulous colour and is a great detoxifier in its own right. Add also the chilli and garam masala and cook for a minute or so. By now it should be smelling very tantalizing.

Stir in the lentils, water and tinned tomatoes. Sprinkle with black pepper and allow to simmer gently for 45 minutes or until the lentils are thoroughly cooked.

Stir in the freshly squeezed lime or lemon juice along with the fresh coriander.

Serve on a bed of brown rice.

NB: You can serve this as a thick soup simply by adding an extra half-pint of water.

Stir-fried Beansprouts

Serves 4
You will need:
A packet of beansprouts/six handfuls
One teaspoonful of sesame oil
One tablespoonful of low salt soy sauce
Half a tin of bamboo shoots, drained and cut
    into fine matchsticks
One large carrot
A thumb-sized portion of fresh ginger
A clove of garlic, crushed
Olive oil
Black pepper

Beansprouts are a staple of Chinese cookery because of their crunchy texture and the fact that they are rich in iron. They also have renowned detoxifying properties.

Being by cutting the carrot and bamboo shoots into matchsticks and grating the ginger.

Now heat the olive oil in a frying pan or wok so that it's hot. Throw in the ginger and garlic and stir fry for a minute or so. Add the carrot and bamboo shoots and keep stirring.

After a few minutes, toss in the beansprouts and the black pepper and stir for two to three minutes.

Finally, mix the soy sauce and the sesame oil together and drizzle over the dish and serve immediately.

Stuffed Peppers
Serves 2–4

You will need:
75g cooked brown rice
Four red peppers
A generous slice of goat's cheese
One clove of garlic, crushed
A generous handful of fresh basil leaves
Olive oil

Wash the peppers and cut them in half lengthways, removing all traces of stalk and seeds.

Place face up on a baking tray and cook at 180°C (gas mark 4) for a few minutes so that the peppers soften slightly.

Mix the cheese, rice, basil and garlic in a bowl and then fill the peppers with the mixture.

Drizzle with olive oil and replace in the oven, cooking for around 15 to 20 minutes.

Serve with a green salad.

Tomato and Bean Stew

You will need:

One large can of red kidney beans (canned are allowed because dried kidney beans are notoriously difficult to cook correctly)

One large can of tomatoes (or use three tomatoes fresh and peeled – the can is for convenience)

Two onions

Three carrots

Two sticks of celery

One large leek

Two garlic cloves, crushed

300ml stock

Black pepper to taste

700g potatoes

Olive oil

Preheat the oven to 180°C (gas mark 4). Heat a couple of tablespoonfuls of oil in a large casserole dish while you chop up the onion. Sauté the onion for about five minutes, but don't let it go brown.

Meanwhile, chop up the carrots, celery, leek and add in along with the garlic. Cook for around five minutes.

Now drain the kidney beans and add, then pour in the tomatoes, juice and all, and season with pepper. Mix well.

Slice the potatoes and arrange them across the top of the mixture, sprinkling pepper between each layer.

You can now add a little butter or brush the surface with some milk, before putting in the oven and allowing to cook for two hours.

Remove the lid and allow to cook for a further 30 minutes, until the crust is nicely brown.

Vegetable Hotpot

You will need:
One aubergine
Half a dozen okra
250g frozen garden peas
250g green beans
Four courgettes
Two onions
450g potatoes
One large red pepper
One tin of skinned plum tomatoes, without
    added salt or garlic
150ml vegetable stock
Four tablespoonfuls of olive oil
Three generous handfuls of fresh parsley
One tablespoon of red paprika

For the topping:
One courgette
Three tomatoes

This bountiful-looking dish is very warming on a cold winter's day thanks to the paprika.

If you have other vegetables in the house, feel free to mix and match the recipe.

Begin by boiling the potatoes, as always trying to retain as much of the skin as possible.

Preheat the oven to 190°C (gas mark 5).

Now slice the okra in half lengthways and dice the aubergine. Wash and slice the courgettes and top and tail the green beans, throwing them in with the potatoes for a couple of minutes to blanche them. Finely chop the onions, de-seed and dice the pepper, and dice the aubergine.

Now place all the vegetables in a casserole dish. Stir gently with a wooden spoon.

Add the tinned tomatoes, sauce and all, the stock, olive oil, chopped parsley and paprika.

Stir gently again and layer the top with the sliced tomatoes and courgettes.

Cover and cook in the oven for 60 minutes.

Serve while piping hot.

White Fish Terrine
Serves 4

You will need:

450g fresh white fish
(such as haddock or whiting. Ask the fishmonger to remove the bone and skin for
you. (NB: don't ever buy fish on a Monday
as it will not be fresh, there being no catch
on a Sunday. Many traditional fishmon-
gers do not open on a Monday for this
reason)

900ml fish stock
(relax, you can buy fish stock cubes – just
make sure you choose a low salt variety)

25g organic unsalted butter

25g plain flour

Three tablespoons of goat's or sheep's milk

Two free range, organic eggs

85ml organic crème fraiche or natural
yoghurt

A generous handful of fresh parsley

Four tablespoons of wholemeal breadcrumbs

One lemon

Black pepper to taste

This makes a tasty, elegant lunch – no one would
ever guess you were on a detox diet. Also it's rich in
omega-3 oils, and be made in advance.

Preheat your oven to 160°C (gas mark 3).

Poach the fish in the stock until tender.

Retaining the cooking liquid, remove the fish and mash with a fork until smooth.

Melt the butter in a saucepan, add the flour and stir continuously over the heat for about a minute.

Mix the milk with approximately five tablespoons of the fish stock and add this to the flour and butter, stirring all the while.

Now add the mashed fish.

Separate the egg yolks from the white. Beat the yolks, adding the crème fraiche or yoghurt and the juice of the lemon, black pepper and perhaps a dash of anchovy essence for extra flavour.

Add to the pan, along with the washed and chopped parsley.

Whip the egg whites until thick and opaque and fold into the dish.

Pour the breadcrumbs into a well-oiled loaf tin and add the mixture.

Cover with foil and bake in a bain-marie* for approximately one hour when the dish should have set and risen.

*a bain-marie, literally 'Mary's bath', means placing the tin in a larger vessel full of water. It ensures that the dish is cooked gently.

Wholewheat Penne with Pesto and Cherry Tomatoes
Serves 2

You will need:
150g wholewheat penne
Two handfuls of cherry tomatoes
Two tablespoonfuls of organic pesto
One onion
Olive oil
Black pepper to taste

This is a very simple, fresh tasting and nutritious dish, which will give you plenty of slow-release energy. Ideal for a special lunch or a light evening meal.

Begin by cooking the penne in boiling water. Don't add salt to the water, though a dash of oil will help prevent the pasta from sticking together.

Detox

Chop the onion and sauté till transparent in the heated olive oil. Don't let it turn brown. Now add the pesto, stirring it in to make a paste.

Drain the pasta. Stir in the washed whole cherry tomatoes to the pesto sauce, ladle the sauce over the pasta, and serve.

Desserts

Apple Custard
Serves 4

You will need:
Three good-sized Bramley cooking apples
150ml water
A good pinch of cinnamon
Two free range organic eggs

Set the oven to 180°C (gas mark 4).

Place the water, cinnamon, and peeled and chopped apples into a saucepan and heat on a low heat until the apples begin to soften into a thick puree.

The cinnamon helps to take away the bitterness of the apples – but if you feel you would like more sweetness, instead of sugar, add a handful of currants.

Now pour the mixture into a blender, adding your two whisked eggs a little at a time.

Once the mixture is truly blended and smooth, pour into a 20cm baking dish and cook for 25–30 minutes.

It should be golden on top and firm to the touch.

Baked Pears

You will need:
Four ripe pears
Four tablespoons of cooked buckwheat
100ml blackberry or raspberry juice – if you cannot get your hands on either, use a tinned variety, so long as it is tinned in fruit juice and not syrup. The berries themselves can be reserved for another dish or used as part of the pear stuffing
A good pinch of cinnamon
Four cloves
Some freshly grated nutmeg
Olive oil

This is a delightfully spicy dessert, particularly suitable at Christmas time and a lot less toxifying than the traditional Christmas pudding.

Preheat the oven to 180°C (gas mark 4)

Halve the pears lengthways, taking out the seeds and some of the flesh. Put the flesh to one side.

Mix this with the buckwheat, nutmeg and blackberry or raspberry juice till it is moist.

Keep a little juice aside for later.

Fill the pears with the mixture and place the two halves of each pear back together again.

Smooth a little olive oil over the skins and then sit

the pears in an oven dish so that they don't collapse or open up.

Now sprinkle with a little cinnamon and stick a clove in the top of each.

Pour the remaining juice into the dish and baste the pears every now and then as they cook for ten to 15 minutes.

Banana and Almond Cream
Serves 4

You will need:
200g fresh tofu
200g bananas
75g shelled and ground almonds
Pinch of cinnamon
A small handful of almond flakes to garnish

This has a lovely creamy texture and takes minutes to make.

Simply mash the bananas and tofu together and then liquidize for a minute or so to get a really smooth paste. Spoon into dessert dishes and allow to chill

Just before serving, sprinkle on a little cinnamon and a couple of almond flakes.

Banana Crumble
Serves 4

You will need:
Four bananas, the riper the better – even black ones will do
100g porridge oats
One tablespoon of tahini
Some flaked almonds

Greengrocers often sell overripe bananas cheap so next time you see some, buy a bunch and make yourself this fantastically sweet, comforting pudding.

Begin by mashing the bananas and placing this mixture in the bottom of an ovenproof dish. You don't need to add any kind of sweetener because overripe bananas are very sweet naturally.

Now mix the oats and tahini and spread evenly over the banana.

Sprinkle over the flaked almonds and cook at 160°C (gas mark 3) for around 20 minutes.

Serve alone or with a dollop of fresh natural yoghurt instead of cream.

Yoghurt Ice Cream
Serves 4

You will need:
250g soft fruit – berries, peaches, plums or
    nectarines
One teaspoon of honey
300g natural yoghurt

This isn't really ice-cream but it is superb and melts in the mouth.

Wash and de-seed the fruit and then place it in the blender and liquidize it, along with the honey, until it is really smooth.

There are two ways to do this: you can add the yoghurt now and freeze the lot for two to three hours.

as the various fruit juices will 'bleed' into the yoghurt.

If you want a colour contrast – the colours of the fruit standing out against the white of the yoghurt – then freeze the fruit first for around two to three hours. Remove it from the freezer and break into small pieces, add it to the yoghurt, and freeze again for two to three hours.

As with regular ice-cream, remove from the freezer 10 to 15 minutes before serving.

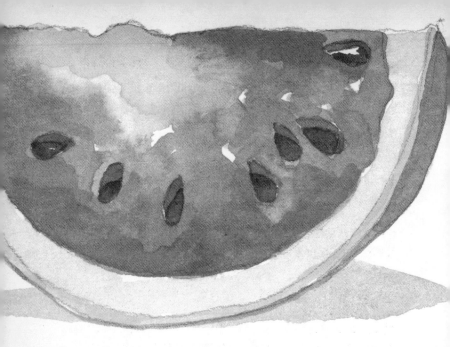

The Liver

WEIGHING in at 1.5 kg, the liver is the largest organ in the body. It produces and secretes bile and 1.7 litres of blood flows through it every minute of every day.

Without it, you would die and without it functioning normally, you are looking at a whole host of health problems.

There are two veins that 'feed' the liver. The hepatic artery, a single vein that spreads itself across the liver in dozens of tiny capillaries, brings blood rich in oxygen and nutrients to the liver. Once these ingredients are absorbed, the blood is taken away to the heart and lungs for re-fuelling.

The portal vein brings nutrients extracted from food passing through the intestinal tract to the liver.

In return for all this feeding, the liver has a huge list of functions.

The great detoxifier

The modern world is a toxic place, particularly the urban part of it. Even on an organic diet, with loads of exercise and deep breathing thrown in, we absorb a giant cocktail of bizarre, unwanted chemicals every day of our lives, be it from the exhaust pipes of passing cars to the by-products of using a spray-on deodorant in the mornings.

This junk has to be processed somehow, otherwise it would just circulate round our bodies endlessly, building up and up. The liver does the processing, breaking these substances down so that they can be safely excreted.

The liver also processes two of our most popular, and voluntarily ingested toxins: alcohol and cigarettes. But give it too much to work on and it will not be able to cope.

Alcohol

Increasingly, alcohol functions as a form of social glue. We meet our mates in the pub, when we have something to celebrate we toast it with a glass of champagne, when Christmas looms we stock up on wine and beer because we know we'll have visitors, and only the most miserable of humbugs would have a dry house at that time of year.

And this is fine. So long as we know when our body has had enough.

Health guidelines suggest a maximum of 21 units per week for women and 28 per week for men, ideally spread over the days with one or two days off in between.

Aim for around two to three drinks (that is, units – half a pint of beer, one small glass of wine, a single measure of spirits) a day. If you find this difficult, try making a short drink into a long one by topping it up with tonic or orange juice. Or alternate an alcoholic drink with a soft one.

Some people find it impossible to resist drinking too much when they find themselves in a social situation – in which case, perhaps you should consider curbing your social commitments. It may seem like a drastic step but it is for the benefit of your health.

If you are concerned that you might lose touch with friends, find ways to socially engage that don't involve alcohol. Suggest a night at the pictures, or invite them round for dinner at your house where you can take more control over how much you drink.

Don't fool yourself that by drinking a lot of water afterwards you can bypass the harmful effects of alcohol. It will make you less dehydrated, but the toxins have still been ingested and still have to be got rid of.

The reason we have to be so careful with our alcohol intake is that consistent overindulgence can kill your liver, which, quite simply, means the end of you too.

Ethyl alcohol, also known as ethanol, is the main active ingredient in most alcoholic drinks and is made from the yeast fermentation of starch or sugar. To give drinks their unique flavours, other substances, called cogeners, are added. These are generally believed to be what causes the hangover.

Alcohol is a strong diuretic, which explains why, the morning after, you are very thirsty and have a headache. Drinking a pint of water after you have been drinking can help to alleviate this a little.

Though it is a carbohydrate, alcohol provides only 'empty' calories – that is, it has almost no nutritional value whatsoever. Even organic wines and real ales have nothing to contribute nutritionally, despite the wholesome marketing.

When you drink alcohol it is absorbed very rapidly into the bloodstream. More rapidly if consumed on an empty stomach as food in the stomach can literally soak up some of the drink and prevent it hitting the bloodstream quite so quickly.

Once in the body, a very small amount of alcohol is expelled by the lungs – which is why suspected drunk drivers are tested with a breathalyzer.

However, the burden of expulsion falls largely on the liver, which must break it down so that it can be excreted.

While it is thus occupied, the liver cannot attend fully to any of its other vital functions – which is why you often feel bilious and tired after drinking.

Prolonged overindulgence in alcohol can enlarge the liver and make it fatty, while one in five heavy drinkers develops cirrhosis. This condition can lead to liver cancer or fatal liver failure.

Cigarettes

Assuming you haven't been living on Mars for the last decade, you will know that smoking is not a health-giving habit.

Sadly, that doesn't prevent the number of smokers from rising year on year, particularly amongst women and teenagers.

We smoke for all kinds of reasons: because it makes us feel happier – back in the 1920s doctors actually prescribed them to depressed housewives; because they suppress our appetite; because our friends smoke; because it looks 'cool'; or because it gives us something to do with our hands.

Sadly, there is payback for all this.

Smoking reduces our lung capacity, exposes our body to thousands of toxins per cigarette, and strips us of vitamins.

The liver, responsible as ever for eliminating these aforementioned toxins, doesn't like us smoking any more than our lungs do. It particularly doesn't like the fact that, in order to process the cyanide present in cigarette smoke, it must use up its reservoirs of vitamin B12. Wholegrains, lean meat and fish can put some of this back but wouldn't it be better to cut out the middleman and simply stop smoking?

Other drugs

Drugs, whether the kind bought from a drug dealer or those prescribed by your doctor, all put a strain on the liver, which has to break them down and make them ready for excretion.

If you have had to take a course of drugs for medical reasons or are trying to/are already in the process of dealing with a drug addiction, your liver will need a lot of care and attention.

But watch out for the more everyday drugs too.

An innocent looking cappuccino is rich in nasty little toxins, as is tea and chocolate. Even the decaffeinated varieties should be avoided.

Fat digestion

Fat is insoluble in water. Which means that, when you eat it, you need something to help you digest it — otherwise it passes through your system undigested and therefore without providing any nutritional value whatsoever. And while this may sound like a good thing to those of you who equate fats in food with body fat, believe the entire medical profession when it tells you it isn't.

Without the essential fatty acids, as the word 'essential' suggests, your body cannot function and you die. They are needed for the nervous system to function, for cells to be built and repaired, for blood to clot and the brain to perform.

But eating them isn't the whole story – you need to be able to break them down and extract the goodness from them, and this is where your liver comes in.

To facilitate fat digestion, you need bile and this is what the liver secretes. When you eat, bile is transported from the liver to the duodenum at the top of the smaller intestine, where it assists in breaking fat globules down into smaller and smaller globules. In brief, bile acts like an emulsifying agent, breaking down oils and fats into droplets.

These tiny globules, because they have a much larger surface area in total than the larger globules, make it easier for the extraction of nutrients by gut bacteria before the fat leaves the digestive system and is excreted.

When you are not eating, bile secreted by the liver is stored in the gall bladder from whence it is transported whenever it is needed. If too much is stored there for too long, gall stones can be the result. A healthy liver produces up to half a litre of bile per day. Some of this is excreted along with other waste products and accounts for the colour of human faeces. Without bile, our stools would be a whitish-grey colour.

The remainder of the bile is reabsorbed into the liver. This process is called the enterohepatic circulation and occurs roughly six to eight times a day, depending on how often you eat.

Protein digestion

Your liver is enormously important to protein digestion – in fact, 95% of the proteins found in the bloodstream are synthesized by the liver.

Albumin is one of them and low amounts of it in the blood indicate that the liver is diseased or in some way damaged. Albumin is extremely important as it regulates fluid levels in the blood. Too little of it can cause a severe imbalance, sometimes manifesting itself as fluid retention.

Proteins are also necessary for regulating a healthy blood pressure and ensuring the blood remains suitably viscous without being too thick.

Another protein function is to bind with substances such as vitamins and minerals and transport them to the areas of the body where they are required.

When a protein is finally broken down in the gut

into amino acids, ammonia is released. Ammonia is a highly toxic substance, which your body really doesn't want to have hanging around. Again the liver comes to the rescue, extracting ammonia from the blood as it passes through via the portal vein, and converting it into much less toxic urea.

Glycogen

The level of glucose in your blood is raised every time you eat. This effect is even more pronounced when you eat something sugary.

Some of it is utilized by the body for energy and the surplus is dealt with in two ways.

The pancreas produces insulin, which helps to lower the glucose level, and any left over is converted into glycogen and stored in the liver and muscles. This can be called upon later as an energy source when blood sugar levels start to dip. Thus the liver functions as an important regulator of blood sugar level.

Kupffer cells

Kupffer cells act as the liver's mine-sweepers. They clear out all the rubbish – the dead cells, unwanted proteins, potential allergens (a sudden susceptibility to foodstuffs may be down to an unhealthy or overloaded liver), toxins and used hormones.

Other liver functions

The liver processes lactic acid, the by-product of the old 'fight or flight' syndrome described earlier in the book. If the liver did not do this, the body would be left in a state of high anxiety and, if you feel that you are more tense and uptight than usual, it could be down to a sluggish liver.

The liver also stores vitamin A, which is important for eyesight and in particular, night vision, vitamin B, iron and copper, and produces substances to allow them to be transported to where they are needed in the body.

How healthy is your liver?

The liver is a magnificent piece of biology. It works incredibly hard, adapting to all kinds of situations and foodstuffs and yet it is also incredibly resilient and capable of repairing itself over and over again.

But it can take only so much abuse and, like anything, how much is too much varies from one person to the next.

Constipation can be a symptom of a liver unable to produce enough bile to stimulate sufficient peristalsis, the action of the intestines as they pump waste products out of the body.

If you don't go at least once a day – and you should really be producing stools two to three times a day – you could be suffering from mild constipation.

Headaches can also be a symptom of constipation, caused by a build-up of toxins in the body. The increase in fibre that the detox plan requires will help enormously.

Indigestion is another of those common complaints that could be down to a sluggish liver.

Without sufficient bile to aid digestion, the typical symptoms of indigestion can occur – nausea, bloating, flatulence and trapped wind. It is no coincidence that these symptoms occur most frequently at times like Christmas, when we eat more than usual amounts of rich, fatty food, drink more than our fair share of alcohol and fail to take much exercise.

A plain detox diet can do wonders for indigestion sufferers.

Another symptom to watch out for is halitosis, also known as bad breath. Of course, a common cause of this is dental problems. A failure to keep your teeth clean can result in the kind of mouth no one wants to get close too.

Excessive amounts of coffee, alcohol and cigarettes can also contribute to a sour mouth.

But digestive problems can have another source and the most likely one, when you've ruled out the other two, is a sluggish liver. If your liver cannot cope with its load of food substances, they may remain partially digested and prone to producing unwanted chemical reactions, causing the release of unpleasant gases and toxins within the body.

And where is it going to go?

Rather gruesomely, much of it may come back out of your mouth, causing the kind of odorous breath that makes people back off in droves.

An increase in allergic reactions may also be due to a tired liver.

After all, it is the organ responsible for breaking down potential allergens and, when it is failing to function efficiently, it may be unable to do this effectively. This means you suddenly cannot cope with certain foodstuffs or your skin reacts badly to something it has never reacted against before.

Headaches can also be caused by allergies, so take note of any increase in occurrence.

They may have another cause of course, but improving the health of your liver could alleviate this problem.

Watch out too for a prolonged dip in your energy levels. As the liver is responsible for maintaining a regular blood sugar level and processing glycogen, it stands to reason that, if it's not working well, you are going to be more tired than usual.

On a more serious note, heart problems can have their root in a failing liver. Basically, if your liver cannot digest fat properly and this results in there being too much of it in your bloodstream, your blood will become more viscous. This makes for more work for your heart, whose job it is to pump blood round your body, perhaps causing it to become overloaded.

A higher fibre diet, packed with fresh fruit and vegetables, can go a long way to helping your liver overcome this problem.

Your health check list

Keep a health diary for a month, noting any occasions when you suffer:

Headaches
Indigestion
Constipation (that is, not having a healthy
   bowel movement more than once a day)
Flatulence/trapped wind
Bad breath/coated tongue

Take a good look at your skin, which serves as one of the very best monitors of your state of health. Despite what the so-called 'scientists' who sell face cream may tell you, flaky, spotty, dull skin has a lot more to do with what's going on in the inside than what you're slapping onto it from the outside.

Conditions such as acne, though not caused by a sluggish liver, can be exacerbated by one. Watch out too for conditions such as eczema and dermatitis, which are often the result of allergies – as we know, allergic responses can be minimized by a little liver TLC.

Also take note of how tired you feel first thing in

the morning, during the day and in the evening. Do you find yourself eating as a means of coping with tiredness? Do you keep yourself going with coffees and cigarettes? Do you try to catch up on your sleep at the weekends yet never seem to make good the sleep debt? Do you find physical exercise exhausting?

An inability to lose weight when in the past it has been relatively easy may have its source in liver fatigue. If you consider that the liver is as essential to digestion as a stomach and an intestine, you realize that a hitch in its performance is going to make weight loss diets very tough indeed. That said, unless you exist solely on cigarettes and sodium-laden ready meals, most weight loss plans would help you to detox naturally.

Last but not least, keep a note of your moods. Low moods and mood swings can be caused by poor health, resulting from a sluggish or malfunctioning liver.

You may be surprised by how many of these 'minor' ailments you suffer from on a regular basis. Usually, unless a health problem is very pronounced and debilitating, we tend to ignore it, assuming it will go away of its own accord. Well, it probably won't. But a detox diet might very well help to banish it.

A No-Equipment-Needed
Fitness Plan
(Almost)

THIS seven-day programme is designed to increase your cardio-vascular fitness, tone up your muscles and increase your suppleness. You don't need access to a gym or fitness equipment, though loose clothing and a stout pair of training shoes are essential. The best times to exercise are first thing in the morning or after work, though it has been proved that a series of short bouts of exercise adding up to 30 minutes is every bit as beneficial as 30 minutes flat out.

Day one

Cardio-vascular

Power walking

Power walking has taken a long time to catch on but, because it works and is less injury prone than running, it is now one of the fastest growing leisure pursuits in America.

Begin by walking at a gentle pace for at least three minutes to give your muscles a chance to warm up. Keep your abdominal muscles tight, your back straight, but not like a sergeant major's, and hit the ground with your heel first, rolling down onto the ball of your foot. Push with the muscles at the backs of your legs and pump with your arms.

After a gentle three minutes, speed up to around 3.5 miles an hour. For maximum benefits, include one minute of very fast walking and one minute of striding.

Finish with two minutes of gentle walking to cool down.

Toning

Chair squats

Chair squats are excellent for toning thighs and bottoms. Begin by sitting on a chair with your feet on the floor and your thighs at right angles to your lower legs.

Slide forward on the chair so that your bottom is

at the edge of the chair, keeping your feet a little more than shoulder width apart.

Press the heels into the floor, keeping the abdominal muscles tight and the chest lifted. Now slowly stand up and then slowly sit down again. Don't allow yourself to collapse downwards.

Repeat 12 times.

Inner thigh lifts

Inner thigh lifts, as they sound, are ideal for toning your inner thigh. Lie down sideways on an exercise mat or a blanket folded in two, with your arm tucked under your head for support and your other hand tucked into this arm.

Bend your upper leg and rest the knee on a folded towel while ensuring that your hips are aligned. Now lift the upper leg slowly. You should feel this in your inner thigh – anywhere else and you're doing it wrong.

Repeat ten times for both legs.

Outer thigh lifts

Outer thigh lifts are as outlined immediately above except this time it is your lower leg you fold and the upper leg you lift. Be careful not to lift this leg too high – 12 to 18 inches is fine.

Both lifts are ideal for toning up thighs and will result in a streamlined, longer muscles.

NB: if you are trying to lose weight, you may find that losing fat from your thighs is particularly difficult.

These two toning exercises will benefit you a great deal.

Lying butt squeeze

Lying butt squeeze is designed to tone the buttocks. Begin by rolling onto your back (using a mat to protect the bones of your spine) with your legs slightly apart, your feet flat on the floor, knees bent and arms by your side.

Now contract your abdominal muscles and those in your bottom and the backs of your thighs, giving them a good long squeeze. Slowly lift your hips but not so much that your back is arched.

Repeat 12 times.

Suppleness

Calf stretches

Calf stretches begin with standing upright. Take a small step backward with one foot, keeping the toes of both feet pointing forwards, and give your calves a good stretch. Hold for ten to 20 seconds and repeat five times for each leg. As with yoga stretches, push as far as you can go before it becomes uncomfortable and the next time you try it, you will be that little bit more flexible.

Front thigh stretches

Front thigh stretches require a chair to help you maintain your balance. Gently holding the chair and standing side-on, bring your heel to your buttock, clasping the ankle with your hand. Keep knees slightly bent and try to keep them together. Repeat five times for both legs.

Lying hamstring stretches

Lying hamstring stretches require your mat to lie on again. Lying on your back with both legs bent and feet flat on the floor, raise one knee into your chest. Now slowly extend this leg. You might want to hold your knee in place while doing this.

Hold for ten seconds and release, repeating five times for each leg.

Knee stretches

Finally, knee stretches. Again, start from your lying down position with your knees bent. Raise one knee and lift it diagonally across your chest so that you can rest the foot on the opposite thigh. This will stretch your outer thighs and hips a treat. Hold for a count of ten and repeat five times for each leg.

Well done! That's one day nearer to total all-over fitness.

Day two

Cardio-vascular

If you are feeling a little stiff after yesterday, begin with a five-minute warm-up. This could be as basic as five minutes' brisk walking or marching up and down the stairs at home.

When you feel that the blood is pumping and your muscles are a little looser, you are ready to begin.

Skipping

For skipping you will need a rope of some description. It should be long enough for you to jump over it comfortably so, roughly speaking, you need a length of decent quality rope around twice your height. That said, children's skipping ropes are easy to buy and usually of sufficient length.

Begin by marching on the spot for three minutes, trying to keep to a regular rhythm. To help you along, put on some music with a strong beat. Now take your skipping rope and skip for five minutes, landing on each foot alternately rather than on both feet at the same time. Keep your knees slightly bent and 'soft' rather than stiff and locked. This ensures that the right muscles are doing the work.

A simpler option for skipping novices is to adopt a heel-to-toe action, keeping your feet on the ground. Simply making the actions you would for jogging – that is, shifting the weight from the heel to the ball of your foot with one foot and from the ball of the foot to the heel with the other. Fold the rope to a length of around two to three feet and hold in your hand, rotating it to keep the beat.

It sounds easy but this skipping is a real calorie

burner and will give your legs a good workout.

When your five minutes are up, march for three more minutes to cool down.

Toning
Upper abdominal curls
Upper abdominal curls are excellent for toning up your torso and strengthening the lower back. They are also highly recommended for runners as the action of running compresses the spine and weakens the lower back. This is a good antidote.

However, it is more important to get this exercise right than to do it hundreds of times. Think quality, not quantity.

Begin by lying on your back with a mat or folded blanket to protect your spine. Place your hands gently behind your head, your thumbs at your ears and your fingers spread wide as support for your neck. Alternately, cover your ears with your hands so that your elbows stick out at the sides.

Take a deep breath and, as you exhale, slowly curl upwards, pulling in your abdominal muscles. Curl only until your shoulders lift off the floor and then curl as slowly down again.

Beginners should repeat ten times, while those who are fitter should try for 20.

One good way to ensure you place the emphasis in all the right places is to adopt a 'negative' approach – this means concentrating on the return part of the exercise, rather than the outward journey. In this case, your effort is focussed on the way down, not the way up.

Knee curls

Knee curls are also worthy torso-trainers that should be done carefully.

Lie on your back with your arms by your sides, palms facing downwards.

Take a deep breath and, as you exhale, pull your knees in towards your chest, squeezing those abdominal muscles and keeping your feet together.

Curl only until your bottom lifts off the ground and then slowly uncurl. This has to be done slowly in order to be effective, which means you must avoid letting the natural momentum of the movement do all the work. Combat this by pausing throughout the movement, never allowing yourself to flop onto the mat, no matter how tempting.

Repeat ten times if you are a novice, 20 if you're fitter.

Rear leg lifts

Rear leg lifts will tone up the area at the back of your thigh. Begin by turning over so that you are lying face down on your mat, keeping your legs straight and together and resting your head on your hands for comfort.

Keeping both hips to the floor, slowly raise one leg

a few inches off the ground and then gently lower it back down.

Repeat with the other leg and continue alternating legs for a set of ten or 20 each leg.

Take care not to speed up while doing this exercise. Flapping legs don't make for toned muscles.

Waist shaper

Finally today, the waist shaper which, as it sounds, is great for shaping up your midriff.

Lie on your back again, with legs slightly bent and feet flat on the ground. Put one hand behind your head, with the fingers spread out as before in order to support the neck. Keep the other hand free.

Now slowly curl up and, with the free hand, reach for the opposite ankle. Repeat alternately, either ten or 20 times for each leg.

Suppleness

The invisible tummy tuck

The invisible tummy tuck gives toning and suppleness all in one and can be done virtually anywhere, any time. It is very effective at flattening those troublesome abdominals.

Though it is portable, it is advisable to practise initially in front of a mirror with the palms of your hands against your thighs, just to ensure you are doing it correctly.

Take a deep breath, exhale and, once you have

finished exhaling, draw your waist in as tightly as you can, holding in the tummy for a count of five, imagining your navel being pulled in towards your spine.

Now release your tummy, take a deep inward breath and repeat the movement 20 times.

Try to repeat the movement twice a day and, once perfected, you can practise it while watching television, while seated at your desk or stuck at traffic lights on the way home.

This movement is also good for stimulating peristalsis and is best performed on an empty stomach as you might induce nausea if full.

Day three

You might have sore legs today. That's good. It means the treatment's working. To give them a rest, today's work concentrates on the upper body, which most of us – particularly women – are very guilty of neglecting because we tend to focus on problem pear shapes and forget that strong shoulders and trim torsos can do wonders for our body shape.

The aim is to give you a stronger, more V-like shape. We're not talking body-building here, just a little lean muscle to give your body definition and to increase your metabolism.

Actually, metabolisms vary very little from one person to the next. The difference is in energy expended (which is why fidgety people are thin and sedentary types are fat) and in muscle mass, of which we lose half a pound a year after the age of 30.

Basically, the more muscle you have, the faster you burn calories.

These exercises are designed to tone you up but in such a way as to give you lean and long, rather than big and bulky, muscle. Stretching is particularly important therefore: it literally stretches the muscle. This is why ballet dancers and yoga devotees are lean rather than strapping.

If you don't have 3–5lb weights, use a couple of 500ml mineral water bottles instead, filled with water or sand. If you're really stuck, a couple of 450g tins of baked beans will do just as well. Not that you should be buying such anti-detox products as tins of baked beans!

Cardio-vascular

Today is a bit unstructured, just to prove you don't need a gym or an exercise prescription to get fit. But you do need a clear 30 minutes.

Your activity could be walking to work as, if you're following the seven-day plan, this could be your first day back. Or maybe you could take the dog out for an extended stroll before dinner, fit in some lunchtime swimming or cycling round the park. Make sure it's vigorous enough to get your blood pumping and enjoyable enough to make you want to do it again.

Exercise can be this easy, which is an important lesson to learn.

Toning
Wall press-ups

Wall press-ups are an adaptation of an old army favourite. They strengthen the chest muscles and are surprisingly easy.

Placing your hands shoulders'-width apart against a wall and with your arms straight, stand with your feet apart and your head aligned with your spine.

Squeeze your abdominal muscles and lower yourself against the wall, gently lifting your heels until your chin makes contact.

Then press yourself back up, ensuring that your back and head stay in alignment throughout.

Repeat ten times for novices, 20 times if fitter.

Bent-over rowing

Bent-over rowing is a great back strengthener: keep your knees bent and your back straight.

Gently holding on to the back of a chair with your left hand, bend over so that your back is parallel with the floor and your right arm is by your side. Hold a 3–5lb weight (or one of the substitutes mentioned above) in the right hand.

Keeping your arm close by your side, raise the weight slowly to your chest and then lower it, keeping your wrist and arm in alignment.

Repeat ten or 20 times for each side.

Seated shoulder press

If you want well-defined shoulders, you need the seated shoulder press. Sit up in a chair so that your back is straight, ideally against the chairback so that your lumber spine is supported. Hold your weights, one in each hand, at shoulder height.

Raise the arms slowly but don't lock them at the elbows or when at full stretch. The slowly lower and repeat, keeping feet flat on the ground and your abdominal muscles tight.

Repeat ten or 20 times.

Tricep dips

Tricep dips are quite hard going but they are excellent for defining the backs of your arms – an area that goes flabby on even the fittest of people.

Sitting up in your chair, grab the front edge with your hands and slide your bottom forward so that you're sitting on the edge but with your feet flat on the ground. Distribute your weight evenly between your feet and hands and slowly lower your bottom to the floor, keeping your feet flat. The slowly raise yourself again, keeping your back straight.

Do ten or 20 of these as before.

If you find this exercise too difficult, start off with small dips and work your way up.

Stretching

As on day one do knee, lying hamstring and front

thigh stretches; also do the back stretch, as follows.

Sit with your knees on the floor and your bottom resting on your heels. Lean forward from the hips, stretching your arms and back in front of you in a Muslim praying position.

Walk your hands forward to give your lower back an extra stretch. After a hold of 15–20 seconds, slowly walk them back and sit upright.

Repeat five times.

Day four

During your work-out, try focussing on the muscles you are using as you use them. Why? Because it will make the exercises much more effective.

Strange as it may seem, studies have shown that even thinking about exercise makes you fitter, even if you're not doing very much of it. As you lower yourself into a lunge, really concentrate on those thigh muscles, feel them work and stretch, and as your heart rate rises during your aerobic exercises, think of your lung capacity increasing, of all that extra oxygen going into your blood and your muscles warming up like a finely tuned engine.

Not only will this heighten the effectiveness of what you are doing, it will increase the likelihood of your doing the moves correctly and make your workout seem to pass that bit quicker.

Cardio-vascular
Step

Remember Step? It was the exercise craze of the mid-1990s because it got you fit fast. But we tired of tramping up and down on little plastic steps and, like so many fads before it, it went out the window.

But varying your fitness routine is a must and not just because of boredom . If you do the same stuff day in, day out, your body will get used to it and you will reach a fitness plateau. To progress, you need to give your body a shock. And what's more shocking than a stomping step routine to the strain of some pre-millennial disco muzak?

If you don't have a plastic step lurking in a cupboard somewhere, use anything sturdy and around four inches high. A box will do just fine. Brace your 'step' against the wall for stability.

Warm up by marching on the spot for three or four minutes, then face your step and step up with your right foot, placing the whole foot on the step.

Bring your left foot onto the step so you have both feet together before stepping down with the right foot, following with your left.

Repeat, leading with the right foot for four minutes, then lead with the left for four minutes.

Keep your hands either on your hips or pumping in time with the steps. Expert steppers should use their weights and do shoulder presses as they work.

Finally, cool down with a two to three-minute march.

Toning
Standing lunges

Standing lunges work your bottom and thighs like nobody's business. Stand tall, side onto the back of a chair, gently holding it for support.

Take a deep stride backwards with your outer leg and press the heel of your inner leg into the floor. Raising the back heel and keeping your abdominal muscles tight, lower the inner knee until the thigh is at right angles to the floor. Slowly rise up again, bringing the back foot into line with the front one, shake your legs and repeat for the other side.

Do a set of ten or 20.

Leg lifts

Leg lifts work the outer thigh muscles, so give them your maximum attention for maximum results. Stand tall as before, transferring your weight to the leg nearest the chair. Keeping knees parallel and hips aligned, lift the outer leg to the side, leading with the heel. Avoid swinging the leg as you are aiming for a lift distance of no more than 18 inches, and slowly return to stand position. Repeat ten times for each leg.

Tip: keep one hand on your abdomen to ensure you're keeping the muscles tight and your torso aligned throughout the exercise.

Standing thigh crossover

The standing thigh crossover is a very balletic

exercise, designed to tone the inner thigh. As before, concentrate on the muscles you are using.

Standing tall, transfer your weight to the outer thigh, keeping hips level and abdominal muscles tight. Leading with the heel, lift the inner leg slowly across the front of the body, keeping your knee slightly bent and your spine very straight.

Once you have achieved your maximum stretch, return leg to standing position and repeat ten times for each leg.

Waist shaper

When doing the waist shaper, think about whittling away those unwanted inches round your midriff. Sitting upright in a chair, fold our arms across your chest and slowly rotate the upper half of your body, leaving your hips where they are, to the right.

Slowly return to the middle and rotate to the left. Repeat ten to 15 times for each side.

Suppleness

Repeat the routine for Day Three but try to hold each stretch for ten seconds longer.

Day five

Today we're going to take a leaf out of Jane Fonda's book and go for the burn. Despite being a little discredited (pain never did anyone any good), Ms

Fonda's passion for pushing your body to the limits wasn't all that misguided.

If you want to raise your fitness levels and burn up fat, you have to put your heart into it.

If possible, have a pair of stout trainers and some thumping disco music on hand. Recent research found that tracks such as 'Eye Of The Tiger' and 'Flashdance' really *are* motivating, so even if you feel a little self-conscious working along to such overused movie tunes, maybe you should give it a go.

As ever, keep your head and spine aligned, because this helps ensure that all the right muscles are doing the all the right work.

What's more, if you practise holding in your tummy, the muscles there will eventually strengthen.

Cardio-vascular

Warm up for your impromptu aerobics with a two to three-minute march, remembering to keep the abdominal muscles tight and the head and spine erect.

Take care to place the whole foot on the ground rather than just the toes. Pump your arms as you march and make your movements dynamic. This makes it more fun and also makes the exercise more effective.

Gradually step a little wider, making your movements larger, and then move back towards the centre.

Now stop and stand with your feet together. Bending the knees slightly, step your left leg out to the side, hold for a beat, and step it back in.

Repeat ten times for each leg, keeping your hands on your hips throughout.

Repeat the exercise from start to finish, this time lifting the corresponding arm as you go.

If you want to increase the intensity, when your leg comes back to the middle, bend down into a squat for two beats and slowly stand up again.

Repeat for ten or 20 each side.

Now march again, lifting your knees higher.

Now stop with your feet shoulders' width apart. Step to the left, then follow with your right, so that you are standing around 12 inches left of where you started from. Tap with your right foot and move it back to the centre, followed by your left foot.

Repeat to the right, then to the left, for 20 each side. Then march, gradually moving into a slow jog. Slow to a stop and raise your left knee, keeping it lower than hip height, and touch the left ankle with your right hand.

Lower your left knee and repeat for the right. Repeat alternately for 20 each side.

If you can't quite reach your ankle, don't worry; just reach as far as you can without straining.

Finally cool down with two to three minutes of marching.

Toning
Repeat Day One's lying butt squeeze and the inner and outer leg lifts. Also repeat Day Two's upper abdominal curls and waist shaper.

Suppleness

As yesterday, again trying to maintain holds for a longer count (ten at least) than previously.

Day six

Cardio-vascular

As for Day One, get with the power walking.

Toning

Repeat Day Three's tricep dips for one or two sets of ten.

Alternate knee lifts

Alternate knee lifts strengthen the muscles around the knee – a must if you run or power walk.

Sit upright in a chair, keeping your abdominal muscles tucked in and your spine and head aligned. Keeping one leg bent with the foot firmly on the floor, gently raise the other a few inches from the floor and, as slowly, lower it again. Repeat five times then switch to the other leg.

Isometrics

Finally for today, a few isometrics, which are tiny movements designed to be repeated often – they really can do wonders for your body shape. So long as you remember to do them!

Detox

Bottom shapers
Focus on your buttocks, tightening them for ten seconds, repeating the move 20 times.

Thigh shapers
Standing up, tighten thigh muscles for ten seconds, repeating 20 times.

Tummy tighteners
Sitting upright, contract the muscles of your abdomen and press your back against the chair. Hold for ten seconds and repeat 20 times.

Suppleness
As before, keeping working those hamstrings and calf muscles, holding for as long as is comfortable. These exercises should be second nature to you now, so fit in a few extra stretches while you're brushing your teeth or watching television.

Day seven

Cardio-vascular
Skipping
Today you're skipping again, but this time you're going to up the pace a little.

March for two to three minutes as a warm-up. Beginners should now extend their simulated skipping by three to five minutes. Or try two to three minutes of real skipping through their work-out.

Advanced skippers should add six to eight minutes to their workout. You can raise the intensity by adding in a few double jumps or lifting your knees higher with every alternate jump.

Cooling down is important as it helps prevent stiffness and injury, so don't miss out the two to three minutes of cooling down.

Toning
I said no equipment, but you must have a beach ball or a football in the house somewhere. If not, use a cushion.

Beach ball squats
Beach ball squats look effortless but they work your muscles a lot more than you think.

Stand tall with your feet shoulders' width apart. Bend your knees slightly, pull in your abdomen and hold the ball in front of you at shoulder height with your elbows slightly bent. Shift your weight back onto your heels and ensure your knees track over your toes for balance.

Now, using your thigh muscles, do a half-squat as if you were sitting down and then slowly raise yourself up again to a standing position, without locking your knees.

Repeat for a set of ten or 20.

Side waist reaches

Begin as above, this time with the ball held above your head. Keep your abdominals pulled in tightly and gently lean over to one side until you feel the stretch.

Slowly and smoothly return to the upright position. Repeat for a set of ten each side.

Overhead tricep extension

Stand upright with the ball held above the head. Keeping the wrists and lower arms aligned, lower the ball down behind the head without moving the upper arms. Then raise the ball up again without locking the elbows.

Repeat, keeping the elbows in and using the muscles at the back at the back of the upper arms.

Do a set of ten or 20.

Suppleness

This set of stretches can be done from the comfort of your own bed, alternatively, do them on a mat or folded over blanket on the floor.

Hamstring stretch

Lie on your back with one foot flat and the knee slightly bent. Lift the other knee up to your chest.

Keep that knee into your chest by holding the thigh gently or by throwing a scarf or towel over the foot and holding the ends in each hand. Now extend the leg towards the ceiling.

Repeat this exercise gently for both legs.

Whole body stretch
Lie on your back with your feet flat on the floor, your knees slightly bent and your arms by your side. Slowly extend your arms above your head but without arching your back.

Extend the right leg upwards but without swinging it up. You should feel this in your thighs, not your back or abdominals, so concentrate on getting this right.

Switch legs and repeat for the other side, five times for each leg.

Hip and back release
Begin by lying face down. Raise yourself onto your hands and knees, aligning your shoulders with your elbows and your hips with your knees.

Slide your hands forward so your torso forms a long line from your hips to your fingertips. Slowly break that line by lowering your forehead to the floor, making sure your back stays straight. Hold for a count of five, then repeat five times.

Now try extending the stretch by sliding one leg back, keeping the other bent forward with the foot turned slightly inwards.

Repeat five times for each side.

Seated hamstring and inner thigh release
Finally, do the seated hamstring and inner thigh release, which starts from a sitting position. Keeping upright, bend one leg in so that the sole of the foot is

placed on the inside of the opposite inner thigh. Extend the other leg out to the side as far as you can, keeping the foot firmly flexed – that is, leading with the heel, not the toe.

Pull in your abdominal muscles and turn to face the extended leg. Slowly lean forward from the hips rather than the middle of the back, until you feel a gentle stretch in the back and inner thigh area.

Switch legs and repeat for the other side.

Repeat five times for each side.

Well done!

At the end of one week, even the person who hasn't exercised since they last ran round the playing fields at school should be feeling a little more vigorous.

But don't stop here

Take a day off – in fact, days of rest are just as important as days of training, so don't regard it as a lazy thing to do.

Then, once you're rested, get back to it. Vary your routine, adding stints of aerobic exercise into your day as and when you can. Got five minutes? Walk or run up the stairs a couple of times, or take a brisk stroll round the block.

And keep up the toning and the stretching. It is so easy and it will make all the difference.